Visitors From Within

Extraterrestrial
Encounters
and Species Evolution

SECOND EDITION

Visitors From Within

Extraterrestrial Encounters and Species Evolution

Lyssa Royal and Keith Priest

A Royal Priest Research Book

Granite Publishing, LLC
P.O. Box 1429
Columbus, North Carolina 28722

Library of Congress Cataloging-in-Publication Data

Visitors from within: extraterrestrial encounters and species evolution
/ Lyssa Royal and Keith Priest
p. cm.
"A Royal Priest Research Book."

ISBN 1-893183-04-1
1. Human-alien encounters 2. Human evolution
3. Metaphysics. 4. New Age movement. 5. Channeling (spiritualism)
6. Civilization - Extraterrestrial influences.
I. Priest, Keith. II. Title.

BF2050.R69 1999
001.942--dc21

99-17177 CIP

First Printing, March 1992

Second Printing, May 1992

Third Printing, August 1993

Second Edition, February, 1999

Original Cover Artwork: Corey Wolfe
Reproduction of cover art prohibited

Printed in the United States of America.

Granite Publishing, LLC
P. O. Box 1429
Columbus, NC 28722 U.S.A.

www.5thworld.com

Dedication

To all humans who have allowed the abduction
phenomenon to touch their lives...
Thank you for being humanity's pioneers
on the evolutionary frontier.

Table of Contents

Note: This book is a second edition published in 1999. Two new chapters (Chapters 11 and 12) have been added since the first edition, which was first published in 1992.

Preface

In September 1961 Betty and Barney Hill were driving back to their home in New Hampshire from a trip to Canada. During this journey they had an encounter with the unknown. After sighting a flying saucer, they arrived home with two hours of missing time. Barney found scuff marks on the top of his shoes. Betty saw rows of strange, shiny circles on the hood of their car. After months of psychological stress, they finally sought professional help from a distinguished Boston psychiatrist, who conducted many hours of regressive hypnosis on the couple. The accounts were nearly identical; they both revealed an encounter with small, greyish humanoid beings who questioned them and submitted them to a physical examination. The modern era of the UFO abduction phenomenon had begun.

Today, from all over the world, there are literally thousands of reports of human beings who have not only seen a UFO, but have had actual physical contact with the extraterrestrial inhabitants. Some of that contact has been limited to friendly visits from the "little grey guys" or "the tall ones," while others have told horrifying tales of abduction, scientific experimentation and sexual invasion.

These accounts are no longer coming from just the fringe elements of society, and the evidence supporting their validity is now conclusive to all but the most stubborn of skeptics. When one conducts thorough research of available material on the subject, it would be nearly impossible to conclude that the phenomenon of visitations and abductions is anything but very real.

This book explores the abduction phenomenon from a unique point of view. We are not following the path of the strict investigator, who deals only with highly empirical data that often limits the discovery of new ideas. Nor are we approaching it from a purely metaphysical point of view. We are attempting to build a bridge between the investigative and intuitive worlds.

UFOs and visitors do not originate in our reality. Therefore, they do not conform to the *laws* of our reality. To attempt to understand them using *only* the laws of our reality will always keep us at arms length from any significant answers.

We need a new paradigm with which to understand the visitor phenomenon. We already know that our encounters with them break the rules of third-dimensional thought, perception, and reality. We must then look beyond what we know to be true. We must stretch the limits of our imagination in order to break through the walls that divide our reality from theirs. It is only there — in that realm that is as yet undefined — where we will find our answers.

The authors have chosen, at least for this book, not to address in depth the rumors circulating in some UFO interest groups concerning government treaties with negative aliens, reptilian invasions, and similar stories. This "evil alien" syndrome is a distraction that often masks the significance of humanity's encounters with the visitors. For that reason we have not included those perspectives in this work.

The material in this book adds new dimensions to previous perceptions of the visitor phenomenon. One single source cannot provide all the answers, but many sources together can tear the wall down and allow us to see the visitors in a new light. It is time for an expanded vision. It is time we begin to understand.

One of the barriers toward complete understanding is often words and labels themselves. There seems to be no consistent agreement upon the use of labels among those in the ufology community. The authors would therefore like to explain the specific labels we have chosen to use in reference to the abduction phenomenon. We encourage the reader not to become attached to labels, as we use them for convenience only.

Ufology has a tendency to use the labels **Greys** and **Zeta Reticuli** as well as **Intruders** and **Visitors** in reference to the same type of entity. The labels Intruder and Visitor encompass the subjective idea of the experience, whereas Greys and Zeta Reticuli denote a more objectively descriptive facet of the phenomenon. There is not consistent agreement with the use of these labels among those who involve themselves in this field, so we will explain our definitions.

A general description of the entity encountered in this experience can be as follows (other types have been documented that are not relevant for our discussion): The being is generally 3-5' in height (usually 3.5 to 4 feet), and the skin color is various shades of grey, white, or beige. They are usually hairless and the head size is larger in proportion to the body. A very small nose, or none, is usually reported, although some less frequent accounts mention large noses. Very large eyes (usually black) are reported, with seemingly no visible pupil. Males are mostly indistinguishable from females, with no external genitalia evident.

The label **Grey** is probably the most widely used and most general term in use today. We do not use this label because of the heavy negative connotations it carries, which we do not wish to promote. We will address the symbolic merits of the label, however. As mentioned, they do appear in various shades of grey. This idea is quite significant when one considers the energetic orientation of the visitors — neither black nor white. They are generally emotionless and neutral, exhibiting neither benevolence or malice (though many have projected these qualities onto them).

The term **Zeta Reticuli** in reference to ETs was established in connection with two separate contact cases that were both extensively investigated. One, mentioned at the beginning of this chapter, is a very famous UFO abduction case that took place in New Hampshire in 1961. Betty and Barney Hill had an encounter with a UFO and small beings with large heads and large, dark eyes. Betty had repeated hypnosis sessions that helped to uncover some of the memories about this experience. During her abduction Betty was shown a star map by the aliens, which she later reproduced under hypnosis. The map made no sense until several years later when a new star group was discovered. Seen from the southern hemisphere, the star group Reticulum Rhomboidalis (the Rhomboidal Net) fit the description from Betty's encounter. This star group houses the two stars Zeta Reticuli 1 and Zeta Reticuli 2. Since then, many individuals have begun calling those small aliens the **Zeta Reticuli**, or the **Reticulum**. More colloquially, they are known as the **Zetas**.

The second significant account is the William Herrmann case, which began in 1977 and was investigated by Wendelle Stevens. His report was published in 1981. The aliens in this case told the contactee they were from the stars in the Reticulum system. Descriptions of the body types are similar enough to indicate they are of the same (or related) species as those in the Betty and Barney Hill case.

Further exploration of the name Zeta Reticuli yields some interesting results. *Reticulum* is a Latin word that can be defined as "a network of protoplasmic structures, as cells or tissues." This definition is a key element toward understanding our relationship with the abduction phenomenon. This is what they are — a network of bodies, individual cells of an unseen yet single consciousness. These beings do not experience the universe through individual physiology and psychological personalities like humans do. This idea can help us explain their beehivelike or group behavior, which has been observed by so many witnesses.

Zeta, the Greek letter, is where we derive our letter Z — the final letter in the English alphabet. Reticulum, as stated, means "network." Thus the Zeta Reticuli can symbolically mean the "final network." The Zeta Reticuli may actually represent the final network in the tapestry of human evolution.

The authors have chosen to use the label **Zeta Reticuli** to refer to these small extraterrestrials. There is no attachment to the label, and it is used for convenience. The labeling of their origins is of little importance; however, the nature of their consciousness and reality may be of primary importance in the coming decades and centuries.

The term **Visitors** is used frequently in this text and is also preferred because of its neutral connotations. Visitors can be terrestrial or extraterrestrial; they can also be an internal and/or an external phenomenon. The nature of the label Visitors leaves the future open for new and expanded interpretations.

Although many people have experienced this phenomenon as an intrusion into their lives by an external force, we do not consider the term **Intruders** to be appropriate for our purposes. We will not, however, attempt to invalidate the Intruder idea, since this phenomenon is highly subjective and must be dealt with primarily on an individual emotional basis if it is to be resolved. We feel the concept of Intruders sets up a paradigm that does not allow for the dynamic development of thought and emotion leading to the acceptance of personal power and responsibility concerning the abduction experience.

Another significant reason for our choice not to use the term Intruders is that it does not contain the idea of "invitation," which is a key concept in understanding our ideas. We hold the point of view that these abductors are here by our invitation, are visitors, and therefore are our guests. Are we as a species aware of this invitation? Not consciously, apparently. We have segmented our minds into isolated compartments in order to avoid our fears. We often interpret our reality from within houses of trick mirrors in order to avoid who we really are. We frequently refuse to have an honest, direct relationship with our world. Thus they cannot approach us in our world directly. But approach us they will; through the back doors, attics and basements of our minds. *They must come to us through our perception of them.*

These visitors must therefore come to us through the unreal, the realms that we have denied in our daily waking lives — the archetypal and elemental realms, the dream realm, and the realm of our imagination. These realms are quite real to them. How can we deny them entrance into a place that we do not even consider to be real?

The symbolic greyness of the visitors cannot be judged if it is to be understood. The labels of "black and white," "good and bad" are the result of judgment. Through their interactions, they are offering us a chance to venture into our own greyness — a world in which we cannot be comforted by our addiction to judgment. As shades of grey, they are reflecting to us our own greyness — no illusions of black and white, no convenience of right or wrong. This neutral world is filled with demons and fairies, myths, ancient archetypes, modern archetypes, developing archetypes. This is the realm where we are creating our new identity as well as creating the future.

One cannot understand this phenomenon by only looking at those little grey bodies and their crafts. Even analyzing their behavior will not give us a full understanding of what is occurring. We must begin to know the part of ourselves that extended the invitation to them. We must venture into the single unified identity that we are if we are to ever understand why they are here. At least for now, it is our *denial* that determines how they manifest in our lives.

And if we are confused in our perception of the experience, perhaps it is because we are confused about who *we* are.

Introduction

What you are about to read has many implications. At the very least, the authors ask that you consider it symbolic. For those of you whose lives have been touched by the abduction phenomenon, perhaps it is much more than symbolic and is very, very real. Whether symbolic or literal, the material presented in this book is aimed at bridging a gap that lies between the scientific and the intuitive.

This book is a combination of narrative, channeled material, and firsthand accounts. Many individuals distrust, dislike, or fear channeled material and may judge it prematurely. The authors ask that you read it not because it *is* or it *isn't* channeled. Read it because the material presents an alternate point of view. Our sources never claim they have *the* truth. They claim they have information that is meant to be taken as information only — data to be added to the collective human understanding.

The material presented in this book is channeled by co-author Lyssa Royal and is edited only for grammatical and structural reasons. The transcripts are taken from either public or private sessions focusing on the abduction phenomenon. The sources of the channeled material are described below.

Lyssa began channeling in 1985 and was trained formally by a highly respected channel in Los Angeles. Her channeling process has been unique in that she has been committed to pushing her abilities to their limits — into realms perhaps as yet unexplored. It is because of her willingness to stretch her ability that some of this information has been obtained. In 1986 she began the deliberate choice of developing her channeling ability in order to access the quality and depth of information that is presented in Royal Priest Research's first book, *The Prism of Lyra*, and now in *Visitors from Within*.

The channeling process is simple. Lyssa puts herself into a meditative state in which her personality disconnects from her normal perception of reality. Another consciousness links energetically and telepathically with her brain and then uses it as a translation device for the concepts discussed. In no way is she "taken over" by another entity. It is entirely a cooperative process between Lyssa and the entity. It can be discontinued at any time by the choice of the channel. When the session is completed, Lyssa retains only a dreamlike memory of what has transpired.

While in trance, the entities through Lyssa are questioned by co-author Keith Priest and/or various other individuals attending the private or public gathering. The audience questions are in italics and the channeled responses are in normal text.

In no way is it necessary for the reader to believe the entities are who they say they are. It is also unnecessary for the information to be accepted verbatim. Many will agree with the information presented and many will disagree. The presentation of *all* facets of the subject matter is necessary for a coherent and complete understanding of the whole picture.

There are several entities who are channeled by Lyssa in this book. We describe them below because they each have different personalities that will be reflected in the way they present their material.

Germane considers himself to be a nonphysical group consciousness. He claims that he represents a future integrated version of the galactic family of which we on Earth are a part. He often channels about extraterrestrial history, and he was responsible for a large portion of the information in Royal Priest Research's first book, *The Prism of Lyra*. He chose the name Germane because in English it means "coming from the same source." There is no connection with St. Germain.

The term "he" is used in reference to Germane for convenience only. Germane is actually a group, and refers to itself as "we."

Sasha claims to be a physical female from the Pleiades. She is about five feet tall with light-brown shoulder-length hair and large, light-brown, almond-shaped eyes. She calls herself a cultural engineer and specializes in opening contact with planets who are ready to enter the global community. She has had contact with other extraterrestrial races as well as our own, and provides much information about the relationship between different species and the evolutionary patterns of developing planets.

Bashar claims to be a physical male from the Essassani species. The name "Bashar" is a word that has several meanings: "the man" (Arabic), "the messenger" (Armenian), and "commander" (Arabic). He chose that name to reflect several facets of his personality. The Essassani species can also be described as a hybrid species that is a combination of the Earth human and the Zeta Reticuli. Bashar is channeled by only a few people on Earth and infrequently speaks through Lyssa.

Harone claims to be a representative from the Zeta Reticuli species (the visitors). In his work, he is responsible for coordinating some of the genetic research projects the Zeta Reticuli are conducting.

Bringing through channeled material from a Zeta Reticuli entity is quite challenging. The more one delves into the Zeta Reticuli mind, the more it may become odd that Harone, a Zeta, appears to be using quite good English. This is not the case. The Zeta Reticuli do not use English. Their natural telepathic patterns are not even similar to ours. Except for the exchange of the most basic ideas, dialogue between Zetas and humans using vocal English can be rather tricky for both the Zeta and the channel. Channeling them may be very disorienting at first; Lyssa often experiences spinning sensations that cause dizziness.

Harone has spent a considerable amount of time refining his ability to communicate through Lyssa. One-on-one telepathic conversation with the Zeta Reticuli is more common (as seen in documented contact cases), but translating Zeta Reticuli telepathic thought patterns into human patterns and then putting them into English is another matter altogether.

Harone allegedly employs a type of language-translation computer that uses three-dimensional holographic values to assist in the choice of thought patterns most compatible with human thought. They are then translated by Lyssa's brain into near equivalents in English. Lyssa's awareness, her ego, is monitored as feedback by Harone and the computer in order to further refine the communication process. The listeners are also monitored for their conceptualization of the translation. Divisions of the human consciousness (such as the subconscious) are also monitored so the impact of the communication can be better understood by the Zeta Reticuli.

Harone claims he will sometimes have a humanoid present — such as a Pleiadian or an Essassani — to assist in the translation and understanding of the emotional aspects of human communication. The result of the translation into English is brought about by Lyssa, with a very thorough feedback monitoring system that the entities use in order to maintain the clarity of communication.

We trust you will find a use for some of the information presented in the following pages. May a new and optimistic point of view about the visitors be cultivated so that fear may ultimately be transformed into understanding.

1

History of the Zeta Reticuli

"It is their wish to share their knowledge of what occurred in their past so that others will not need to recreate it." — Germane

---

For a clearer understanding of the Zeta Reticuli, one may study the history of their species. This will answer many questions about the Zeta psyche and belief systems. The Zeta Reticuli identity was created from crisis. This idea may account for their baffling methods of communicating with humans.

Presented in this chapter is a brief history of the Zeta Reticuli, channeled from Germane. Audience questions highlight some of the fascinating historical data that is available as we search deeper into some of the aspects of the visitor phenomenon.

* * *

Germane: The primary goal of sharing the history of the Zeta Reticuli with you is so it can allow you to see some parallels between their civilization in the past and yours in the present. There is quite a bit of similarity.

Though the evolution of their race does not really occur linearly, we will place this story in a linear format. We begin "back" hundreds of thousands of years ago in the Lyran sys-

1

tem. The roots of the humanoid race in your area of the galaxy emerged from the Lyran system. The Zeta Reticuli are no exception.

Let us begin in the Lyran system back when civilization was flourishing and new cultures were exploding throughout the cosmos. The range of cultures these early humanoids created was vast. There was one planet we have called the Apex planet that we will refer to as the ancient origin of the Zeta Reticuli race.

This Apex planet was very similar to Earth. The beings on Apex were a mixture genetically just like you are, because the early Lyran races had already begun to colonize. Apex became a melting pot for the genetics of the Lyran races. Therefore their society manifested a great deal of individuality and unpredictability. These qualities were even more pronounced than upon present-day Earth.

There were those who were pacifists. There were those who were warriors. There were those who were technologically oriented and those who rejected technology in favor of an inner spirituality. Every polarity one could imagine was played out on this Apex planet even more dramatically than it is played out on your Earth plane.

Their culture flourished for many thousands of years. However, beneath the surface of the mass consciousness there was a great deal of disharmony because the spiritual growth of the planet did not parallel the technological growth of its inhabitants. The gap began to widen. On the surface of the planet cataclysm began — severe toxicity and severe radiation from atomic blasts even more destructive than on your planet today. There was much pollution. The atmosphere began to deteriorate and plant life was shortly thereafter unable to produce enough oxygen to continue the cycle of carbon dioxide/oxygen which kept the ecosystem balanced.

There were those within the system who were aware of what was happening. They began taking measures to preserve life.

2

They built underground shelters and prepared themselves for the total destruction of the planet's surface. They didn't know whether this was going to occur, but they wanted to be safe. They knew they had a safety margin and that if they were prepared, their race would survive. They began learning to use alternate energy sources that could be used underground without any dependency on sunlight or oxygen from the surface. Thus they created a world that would be totally independent from the surface ecosystem.

Preparation stretched out over many generations. They were farsighted, for they were certain this change needed to occur. They paced themselves and moved slowly. They began to see that they were evolving at such a rapid rate that the Apexian cranial size was quickly increasing. The natural birth process became difficult, for the cranial size was expanding more quickly than the female pelvis could accommodate. Thus there were many deaths during childbirth — of both the mother and the child. Since what you call caesarian delivery was not part of their belief system, they were certainly facing a species crisis.

They were faced with a dilemma. Their population was decreasing. It became obvious that they had to prepare for planetary catastrophe as well as the possible death of their own species. They thus began turning to cloning techniques so they would not be dependent on the birth process. Then they could actually reproduce their species in the laboratory without the need for the reproductive act, conception, or natural birth. They assumed this knowledge would take care of them and they would be ready for anything.

The Apexians did attempt to reverse some of the conditions that were occurring on the planet's surface before they took shelter underground. However, it had progressed too far. Many Apexians were dying from various diseases resulting from radiation or air pollution. They knew this was the time to move beneath the planet's surface.

3

Gradually, individuals wrapped up their business on the surface of the planet and began to inhabit the underground cities. This was a great shock to many. Imagine knowing that you could never look at the sky again...that you could never lie under the stars...that you would be trapped in a rock environment for the rest of your life. Imagine the fear and sorrow these people were experiencing.

Eventually, they all were moved underground. They had to learn how to adapt. Through their cloning capabilities (which they had been working on for at least 100 of their years), they began to understand how a body could adapt to an environment such as this. They began altering their genetics so that when new babies arrived they could be part of the underground ecosystem.

This entailed restructuring bodies so they could absorb frequencies of light beyond the visible spectrum and then change these frequencies into heat. This required a completely different way of body functioning and a new way of teaching the body to absorb nutrients. The bodies began learning to ingest nutrients from some of the luminiferous rocks underground. They had brought from the surface luminiferous plants as well. They studied these plants (which were chlorophyll-based) and allowed themselves to incorporate these qualities into themselves.

All of this occurred over a span of hundreds of years. Many Apexians died. There were successes as well as failures. They eventually got to a point where the population growth leveled out as the death rate decreased. The methods by which they were taking in nutrients and recycling into the ecosystem became symbiotic and balanced. They knew they could survive this way for an indefinite period of time.

While this was occurring under the surface of the planet, profound changes were occurring on the surface. The Apexians did not realize that the planet's toxicity had set a chain reaction in motion. Severe radiation had begun breaking down the planetary energy field on a subatomic level. This created an electromagnetic warp in the time/space fabric surrounding the Apex planet. While they were underground, Apex actually shifted its position in the time/space continuum because of this dramatic subatomic energy breakdown.

Time and space is very much like swiss cheese. A planet in one location is connected through a series of multidimensional networks or passageways to other areas of your galaxy. When this warp began around their planet, the planet was moved through the fabric of time/space to another time/space continuum — which was a significant distance from their point of origin. You have labeled this area the Reticulum star group. The Apex planet was inserted in the Reticulum system around one of the faintest stars in that star group. This occurred simply because the planetary shift followed the fabric of time and space. The underground Apexians were totally unaware of this as they continued with their lives under the surface. They continued saving their species.

If something such as this occurred on Earth, there would be various factions of people living underground who would have no communication with each other. These factions could develop very different cultures over hundreds of years. This is what occurred on Apex. These different factions represent the different variations that have been viewed in the Zeta Reticuli groups. Some individuals say they are very negative; others say they are very benevolent. But it really isn't as black and white as that.

Over the hundreds of years that they were underground, they deliberately manipulated their body type to suit their underground environment. They allowed themselves to become shorter in stature than they originally were so they could make better use of the cavern space. It was merely a conservation effort. Because they were not procreating physically, their reproductive organs atrophied. Their digestive tracts atrophied because they were no longer taking in solid nutrients. They had mutated to allow themselves to take in

5

nutrients through the skin. Their eyes adapted to the environment through the pupil mutating to cover the entire eye. This allowed them to absorb certain frequencies of light beyond the visible spectrum. They had to do this in order to make optimal use of their underground environment. This description of their changes is a general one, since different factions would have made slightly different alterations to their genetic structure.

During this time, they evaluated what they had done to their planet. They concluded that emotions were largely responsible, so they no longer allowed emotion in their lives. They also vowed that they would no longer allow diversity in their culture. Thus they deliberately bred out variations in emotional reactions to differing stimuli. They were adamant that their passions would no longer rule them. They began creating a neurochemical structure in which *every* external stimulus produced the same reaction in every person. They felt this would allow them to integrate into one people and eliminate the warring and passion that had ruled their culture in the past.

Generally speaking, the separate underground factions followed the same reasoning. Most of them adapted themselves biologically in much the same way. This was a natural progression – they were following an equation. But the differences in the factions were more noticeable in their philosophic orientations.

Each faction had differing points of view about their own sense of self. The ones you now call Zeta Reticuli are the more benign and benevolent beings. There are those we can term the "negative Zeta Reticuli" who stemmed from a faction that was interested in gaining power. They carried this desire from their Lyran roots into their mutation. There were other groups whom you have named "the Greys" who were from this Apex world but had slightly different genetic structures. You will find that the extraterrestrials playing a big role in your abduction literature come mostly from this original

Apex planet. This is why there is so much controversy over who is who. Though they have the same lineage, their orientations and motivations are quite varied.

Eventually the Apexians realized that enough time had passed that they could return to the surface of the planet. The atmosphere had not totally regenerated (thus their time on the planet's surface was limited), but they did allow themselves to emerge. When they did, they had quite a shock. Observing the star field, they knew the planet had shifted its position in the cosmos. The stars were very different. The astronomers who had been plotting the heavens during the seclusion were astonished. They realized then what they had done. The more benevolent Zeta Reticuli now were firmly committed to becoming one people and finding out what they had lost during the time they were underground. Thus they diligently learned about the folding of time and space. They didn't even know where they were. They wanted to find out what had happened. They wanted to learn about themselves through other cultures. It was also their desire for no one else to *ever* do to themselves what they had done. At this time, that was their primary motivation.

The other more negative or self-serving groups also emerged on the surface of the planet and realized what they had done. The negative Zeta Reticuli group allowed themselves — with the technology they had in the past — to build ships and move to other planets in the Reticulum system where they built their culture. Others of the self-serving orientation allowed themselves to explore the universe, setting up colonies in several systems including Orion (Betelgeuse) and the Sirius trinary system.

Have any of these beings on Apex been reincarnationally connected with Earth?

Reincarnationally speaking, a good number of them are upon your planet now. Many of these Apexians who died out were somewhat opposed to the idea of manipulating the

Apexian genetic structure. But at the same time, they were adamant about not creating pollution and toxicity and knew the Apex planet had to change. So they have incarnated all through the galactic family — especially whenever they saw a planet coming to the brink of the same kind of destruction they had created in their past. It is their wish to share their knowledge of what occurred in their past so that others will not need to recreate it.

So the Zetas are not indigenous to the Reticulum system?

Correct. However, after Apex shifted into the Reticulum system, the Zetas had many thousands of years of evolution. They have been there so long that Apex is only a dim memory to them.

If the Apexians had spacecraft, why didn't they leave Apex when the catastrophe was occurring?

They could have left had they desired. Understand the nature of their being: They were pioneers; they had the same motivations and passions as the individuals who colonized your America. Even when the pioneers were faced with Indian attacks, they did not want to leave. The Apexians saw this as a great challenge. They felt that by going underground and changing their species, they would heal their past. They felt they would not recreate it again. The majority of them felt that if they left and went somewhere else, they would continue to recreate the pattern. Some of them *did* leave and went to other planets in the Lyran system, but only a small number. For the most part, the individuals who were committed allowed themselves to stay, feeling that this was an opportunity for them to heal their society.

You were saying that the pupil of the eye mutated to cover the whole eye. Does the pupil also grow larger through expanded consciousness?

In their case, yes. The brain was growing larger and there-

8

fore the eye structure as well as their desire for knowledge facilitated the enlargement of the pupil. But they also genetically manipulated it as well. Over a long period of time it would have occurred naturally because the surface area of the eye was not large enough to take in all of the light they needed. Also, the Lyran beings who were their forefathers had larger eyes than the Earth human.

Did the Apex planet move back to its original location once they began healing themselves?

No. The planet still remains in the Reticulum star system. The underground caverns are still home to many of them, though for the most part a good number of them spend time in space on their ships.

Is it possible in our time that our world could create something like this?

Yes, it is. In your current development and use of atomic power, it is not possible, but should you continue using your knowledge of atomics for more destructive means without allowing yourself to evolve from atomics to something else, then you *could* create that scenario.

Understand that there is a certain evolutionary scale (on average) that a civilization will follow. You are now at the stage of playing with the nuclear or atomic energies. There is a natural evolution from atomics that moves you away from the danger point. You are at the point now of almost deciding to move away from the danger scenario. You are still deciding whether or not you are going to take the natural evolutionary process away from atomics.

Most of the Zeta Reticuli that we interact with today are quasi-physical, almost approaching nonphysicality. How did they get to that state? Was it simply the great length of time they've been focused on developing themselves?

The length of time has something to do with it, yes. But also

9

it was because of their technological advancement, which allowed them to evolve themselves physically. They have allowed themselves to evolve to the point where they are on the brink of becoming nonphysical. However, they do not wish to leave physicality because there is still something they think they need to learn.

Never forget that there are different factions of the Zeta beings. Some of them are very altruistic. There are others who are here purely for their *own* reasons and those reasons can be either positive or negative or any shade in between. As an overall idea, they want certain things from you they feel they lack. You see, they think they have made some mistakes in what they have eliminated through cloning. They are now trying to watch *you* and learn how they can successfully integrate these things within themselves.

In a sense we can say that you are their past *as well as* their future. It is as if at every corner they turn, they face you. You represent their past; you also represent their only hope for a future.

2

Zeta Reticuli Revelations

"Your race is allowing itself now to make an evolutionary leap. The Zeta Reticuli are allowing themselves to do the same. Together you will synchronize these leaps into a grand dance."

— Bashar

Anyone interested in the visitor phenomenon has most likely asked themselves the following questions:

1. What type of data are the visitors seeking?

2. Did they experience any unexpected revelations?

3. What have the visitors learned from their experiments?

Slowly, as we begin to understand their psyche, the answers to these questions begin to be revealed. During a large group session, many concerned people voiced their most profound questions. The answers are sometimes shocking in their honesty. Bashar begins by answering overall questions about the visitors. Later, Harone addresses the group personally and candidly about the research conducted by his race, the Zeta Reticuli.

* * *

Bashar: The Zeta Reticuli have been continuing their projects with you by your allowance. They have made some discoveries. They are learning, they are growing, and a portion of their consciousness wishes to share their discoveries with you.

How many different types of Zetas are there? I was under the impression there are dozens.

The answer would be like asking, "How many types of Americans are there?" However, you can lump them into perhaps three broad groups. Within these three types there are tremendous variations. They are not a clear-cut species, as Americans are not a clear-cut group. We use that analogy directly.

The three broad categories represent the following ideas:

1. Straight Zeta. This group will be the Zeta consciousness existing within the outer perimeters of fourth-density reality. Therefore their reality is just barely physical — mostly plasmic in nature. As they are deliberately keeping their vibration from transitioning into fifth density, they cannot interact directly with you except when you are in altered states of consciousness. They cannot enter your physical reality.

2. Altered Zeta. These would be a straight Zeta consciousness altered either physically or in their consciousness to allow themselves to be able to interact with you on the physical plane or in a type of quasi-physical reality. This is the broadest category.

3. Hybrid. A hybrid would be an entity whose primary Zeta Reticuli genetics are combined with genetics from any other humanoid race. This spans many different offshoots and cultures.

The idea that you call the negatively oriented groups are not necessarily placed within these categories we have outlined, though they can be for purposes of illustration. But in a sense, the negative groups have their own categories.

Could you give a briefing for the group here on the Zeta, Harone, who will be speaking, so that when he speaks everyone here will have an idea of whom they are speaking to?

The entity Harone can be considered altered Zeta consciousness. He can enter your nonphysical reality such as the dream state, and can also at times interact with you on the physical level. He is a coordinator (if you wish to call it that) of genetic projects.

I have a follow-up to that. When you say "altered Zeta," do you mean that he is of a hybrid race, or that he has been altered in his own physical body?

He has been altered in his own physical body type.

What would be the nature of that alteration?

It consists of placing the being within an environment of different vibratory frequency from the one that is his natural state. This will allow him to assimilate the new vibration, which is a down-stepping of his vibration, so that he may communicate with you.

Before we speak to Harone, could you address the group briefly and share something about your heritage?

The race I represent, Essassani, has been considered to be a cross between you (human) and Zeta Reticuli. Therefore, in that sense, we consider ourselves to be your children ... birthed from love.

Can you tell us how that cross was achieved?

Understand the idea that though we have our own ancient time line, our own ancient history, the time lines converge at the point at which the Zeta Reticuli concluded their experiments. In a sense, our pasts joined. It is a spiritual evolution, in a sense. We thus have our own ancient history, but we also represent the joining of two races. We represent the idea of integration for those you consider to be the entire galactic family. However, we are but *one* manifestation of the Zeta experiments.

Was there any physical or quasi-physical blending of our DNA with the Zetas' DNA to create your species?

Yes. In the preliminary stages, yes.

What is the purpose and mission of the Zeta contact?

The main focus of their work is multifold. The idea that we wish to stress the most is that they are teaching you about fear. They are allowing you to move through your deepest fears. This allows you in an archetypal way to bring up those fears for transformational clearing. They, in that sense, represent to you the idea of unity just as you represent to them the idea of individuality. You are, in a sense, two opposite ends of a pole, and you are coming together to form one integrated consciousness. You are learning from each other. You are growing from each other. You are giving each other many gifts. Neither one of you are victims of the other. You are all co-creators of the entire experience.

We are speaking of species evolution on a very basic level all the way through to the spiritual level. Your race is allowing itself now to make an evolutionary leap. The Zeta Reticuli are allowing themselves to do the same. Together you will synchronize these leaps into a grand dance. You are, in that sense, mirror images of each other, each choosing to play out the opposite idea. You are discovering your opposites through each other.

Was there a council or governing body who granted permission for the genetic experiments? Or was it a random choice?

Within linear time many of you will understand that there will need to be some type of council in order to "pass a law."

14

But in this case, all is understood on deeper levels, on mass-conscious levels. When they seek you out they cannot interact with you unless you have already given them permission. If any of you in this room have not given them permission, they cannot find you.

So if there is an interaction occurring in your life and you have not yet allowed yourself to totally embrace the idea that it is something you have chosen — that it is something of mutual benefit to both of you — then you might explore your own joining with them by your own choice, by your own willingness to be of service. You either play the role of victim or you do not; there is no middle ground.

They can see you only if you have given them permission to interact. Your mass consciousness at this time has given them permission to seek out those with whom they have formed individual agreements. If you are having contact, you *must* have agreed. This can be a liberating idea if you allow it to be, because once you allow yourself to understand that you have chosen this experience, you thus place yourself on an equal level with them and the nature of your interactions with them will change. You will no longer be a victim. You will be an equal participant. The quality of your interactions with them will change significantly.

This is one of the reasons they are interacting with you — in allowing you to understand that you are not a victim but an equal participant. As each and every one of you allow yourself to heal this rift, you will kick it into the mass consciousness with a critical-mass effect that will allow the entire mass consciousness to view this idea from a different perspective, a different light. You will also assist the Zeta Reticuli mass consciousness to view it in a different light, and thus evolutionary transformation will occur within both species. It is a partnership, always. It always has been, is now, and always will be.

Do you see that we have the same type of agreement with other species beside the Zetas? A cooperative interaction with others toward our evolution?

Absolutely, yes. Your agreements with the Pleiadian races are other examples of evolutionary agreements. All interactions with extraterrestrial races occur because of agreement so that you can learn from each other. There are no accidents.

I have had a lot of conscious contact the last year or two. I just want to comment that I feel such a sense of brotherhood. It is a feeling of love. I get very emotional because when it happens, it is such a wonderful feeling of coming together.

We thank you for your willingness to allow yourself to move through the fear and to be of service by transmitting the vibration of love rather than the vibration of fear. Your service is felt and appreciated.

At this time we will stop and bring through the energy that is called Harone. He will speak to you about many of the discoveries he has made [through the Zeta experiments]. We thank all of you — each and every one of you — for the gifts that you have given by your questions.

* * *

This is the consciousness **Harone**. We will share with you what we consider to be a major discovery we have made. In conversation with several of you through several channels and in interaction with you in dream state levels, we have thus come to the conclusion that we have been searching for emotion within ourselves. For much time we have been searching for emotion. We have bred and cloned emotion out of our species in the belief that it would accelerate our growth and provide us with superior development. We have since understood this was not the case. You on Earth represent a genetic combination that is the closest to our original species. So the interactions we have with you (especially those you call "ab-

16

ductions") are, on one level, our way of observing you. This is in order to learn how to become emotional once again.

Let us address the experience some of you have read about or have had of having probes inserted into your craniums. We wish to tell you that the purpose of this is not for controlling you. These probes are organic in nature and will absorb neurochemicals from your brains. When they are extracted we analyze those neurochemicals. Through that analysis we expect to achieve the ability to simulate your neurochemical secretions. Perhaps if we can simulate these neurochemical secretions, we will thus be able to recapture the idea of emotion.

This is not in any way meant to harm you, to hurt you, to frighten you or to control you — this is something we wish to stress. If you can begin to understand why these procedures are undertaken, perhaps you will allow yourself not to be so frightened of them. Perhaps you will allow yourself to transmute your fear into an active and conscious cooperation with us. This will be of service to us greatly. It will also be of great service to *you*.

In conversations we have had with other species not of your planet and in our analysis of the data received from you, it has become clear that we have indeed discovered the beginnings of emotional development within ourselves, crude as it may be. We have been misinterpreting some of our motivations to be purely mental. We now understand that some of our motivations are not mental at all, but are driven by emotion. Though we do not understand this emotion in its entirety or even in little pieces, we allow ourselves to recognize it as the beginning of an emergence of an emotional body.

This recognition we have made is the recognition that the idea called "curiosity" is indeed an emotional expression on our part and not a mental one. Our motivation, as we have always said, is one of curiosity. But we have mislabeled it as mentality instead of emotionality.

We do not know if you understand the implications of this. For us, this is a milestone. We can understand that all of the work we have done in observing you and in conversation and interaction with other species is an indication to us that we have been successful. Thus it fires our motivation. It fires our curiosity to continue.

We wish at this time to formally thank you for your participation in this experiment and in the growth of both of our species. I speak as a representative of my people. As I speak to you and thank you as a group in this room, know that this gratitude is emerging into your mass consciousness. I speak this as a representative. I speak this with all motivation. You are thanked by us.

You mentioned that you had misinterpreted curiosity to be from your mentality, rather than being emotionally based. Is that analogous to what happens to some people on this planet who are not in touch with their emotions? Do you learn from our experiences in doing that as well as from your biochemical experiments?

It is easier for us to process the data from our biochemical experiments because that type of empirical knowledge is something we can use directly. The data that we get from observing all of you is somewhat more difficult for us to process, though it is still used.

Is there another area in which we could be of service to you? Is there something else we can do to help another area of your exploration?

One of the focuses for us now in observing you has to do with your own sexuality. We do not know if there is one specific thing that you could assist us with; if we knew it, we would be closer to the answer. This may sound intrusive to many of you, but many of you are aware that some of my species will at times observe you while you are engaging in sexual behavior. This has been a source of shame to some of

18

you. We wish you to know that it is not meant as an insult. Those of you who have these experiences have agreed to participate. We can thus find you because of your agreement. Because of your agreement, we will observe.

As for the amount of interaction we have with you sexually, that will be up to the agreements between you as an individual and us as a group. We are told that your fear is a vital part of your transformation. We would request that should you allow yourself to release the fear, should you allow yourself to transmute the fear, you will thus aid us in discovering more about ourselves. We do not know how this will come about, but we do know that we wish to ask you to work on this fear. You are not victims. You never have been.

I had a visit from some Zetas last week who were probing my stomach. I became very upset because it hurt. What was going on?

What area of your stomach?

Around my belly button.

That is a common place. The clinical term would be an extraction of ovum. We repeat, this is not meant to frighten you. You have agreed to this. You can transmute the fear when you are in the experience by placing a very solid blue light around your body, which will lighten or make your field less dense. This will allow us to work with you easier, which will cause less discomfort to you.

I would like to know if I have had this type of contact. I feel sometimes that the contact goes back a long time. Is this actual, or is it my imagination?

It is actual. Your imagination would not fabricate such an experience. Imagination is not the myth it is believed to be. It is a realm of reality. It is a realm through which you allow communication that you do not allow in many other ways. This is a reality.

19

What fear is it in us that needs to be released to allow the evolutionary process to continue?

The fear of what you will become if you follow through. The fear of losing yourself. The fear of becoming *us*. The fear of evolution.

We are told that humans fear the unknown. Yet the unknown is what drives you to face your fears. In this particular case, there is nothing but evolution. Nothing we say can make you understand this. You will need to come to terms with this yourself. *It is the unknown that you fear, yet it is the unknown that drives you on.*

Also, in the experiences there is ecstasy and incredible insight. There is also the horror of the sense of invasion.

Yes. We understand, at least mentally, what you are saying. In our species there is no such thing as the idea of invasion because we see ourselves as all one. We understand that humans have boundaries — you keep yourselves separate. We have also been made aware that you have many levels of consciousness. You call some of them "conscious," "subconscious," and "unconscious." From where we communicate to you, we cannot tell the difference between those layers. So if the subconscious is speaking one thing and the conscious another thing, we hear the loudest voice.

Coming to peace with the idea of invasion is knowing that you *cannot* be invaded; everything you see, everything you experience is part of the same one thing. It is all a reflection of the whole. Nothing is outside of you. It is all a part of you. It is you invading *yourself*. Coming to terms with this and **changing the perception from invasion to communion will be profound indeed.** For it is not an invasion of one to another, but a joining, a communing, an integration. We know that together we will make this species leap...as we hold hands and take the steps together.

You suggested before that the abductee surround themselves in the blue light to make the experience less painful. Has this been suggested by your people when they are working with humans? [More on this in the chapter entitled "Changing the Abduction Experience"].

Yes, it has. Sometimes the blue light is implemented by the person being visited after the suggestion is given, and they assume that *we* have done it. But actually *they* have.

Can you explain why, among the Zetas, you were chosen to be channeled?

As a coordinator of my projects, I am always looking for ways to facilitate the projects in the smoothest way. Through detailed analysis it has come to my understanding that to seek you out in what you call your conscious state (which to you is your more dominant state), we could thus state our intentions and our desires for communication. This would seep into the other layers of your consciousness. So through my research, it seemed logical to communicate with you on the direct level that you value most.

I then spoke to individuals within various organizations such as those you call "the Association" to find out the best way to facilitate this process. It was suggested that there are biological channels who could relay my messages to your conscious minds. Thus the Association sought out channels who have a direct connection to myself or my research group. The humans I speak to—you—have a connection to my group, either being visited in your dream state or actually being worked with physically. This is why I speak to you and not another.

This is a process that can occur without emotions? You don't need emotions to channel through? It seems empathy is necessary on both sides.

Emotions are not necessary to channel, though I am work-

21

ing with physical facilitators on my end. The three of us are linked into a computer device that synthesizes our thoughts. They provide a balance for my thoughts so that the biological vehicle [Lyssa, the channel] can receive them. Thus they are translated.

You said you have two facilitators. Who is the other beside Bashar?

Sasha. [a Pleiadian].

Do you then personally understand the different layers of our consciousness?

I do not understand the intricacies, but I now understand that they exist.

Are our different layers of consciousness a valuable tool for your growth?

We do not know enough about them at this point to be able to understand their value. From our point of view, they seem more a disservice to you than a service, so we have not examined it in its totality. However, it must serve you, otherwise you would not perpetuate it.

As I speak to you, do you understand me on a fuller level than just my conscious thoughts?

Yes. However, part of the reason I have chosen this type of communication is so I may communicate directly with your *conscious* minds. Right now, in this communication your conscious minds speak loudest. The other portions are very dim—*for this communication.* If I need to access other portions of you in order to bring through an answer to one of your comments, my facilitators will assist me with it.

It is our understanding that you do not understand emotions from an experiential standpoint. What is it like for you to be discussing our emotions with us when you do not have an experiential understanding of it?

22

I obtain much of my data through interfacing with my facilitators. The conversation that is shared with you is recorded and I use it for later research. You are communicating with the Zeta consciousness called Harone. But it is tainted with communication or flavoring from the entities Sasha and Bashar.

But the subjects we are discussing about emotion, aren't they an enigma to you?

Some are, some are not. Some are not necessary to experience in order to understand.

When you did away with emotions, was love part of that? Love is so intimately related with God. Where did God fit in?

The past of my race was very similar to yours, but much more extreme. We had severe toxicity, radiation, and societal dysfunction even more than you have. The imminent collapse of our planetary society allowed us to began developing a way that we could survive. We built underground facilities to house our physical bodies and began seeing emotion as the root of our problems. (We are not necessarily saying this is the right thing, but this is what we did.)

Through various things that happened, we were unable to bear children and had to survive through the means of cloning. Because we were becoming adept at cloning, we thus developed a means to clone out neurochemical responses in the brain to various stimuli. Instead of your many neurochemicals, we created one neurochemical that would output to any given stimuli. This created nonvariance in our responses. This ultimately allowed us to develop away from an understanding of ourselves as emotional humanoids and focused us in our mental bodies.

The concept of love, we perceive, is present with us. But it is expressed in a different way than you express it. We understand that we are a whole. We are a joined unit. This unit

23

loves itself unconditionally. We can love every portion of the unit.

I am being told by my facilitators that what we experience is not necessarily love as we think it is. It is more akin to acceptance. I do not know if this is accurate, but this is what I am told. I am also told that we are beginning to have a relationship with the idea of love as we communicate with you. This is another idea for study, for it is not something I am aware of.

What about God? Was God eradicated along with emotions?

God was focused in a different way. We became an aspect or an integrated version of God. But God became, in a sense, less expansive.

It was with great surprise about a month ago that I suddenly realized I had participated in some of your genetic projects. I actually perceived I had produced a fetus that was taken by you. Could you discuss this process?

We will discuss the process of the creation of fetuses, though it is our understanding at this point that we shall not validate the truth on an individual level. This is because the discovery of the truth of this for each and every one of you (if applicable) is important for your growth.

For those females who have made agreements in this process, there are several things that may occur. You may simply provide genetic material such as ova to us for further research. Some of the ova are joined with sperm. Some are used for other cloning processes. Sometimes just skin scrapings can provide the DNA structure that we are looking for. Other females are impregnated with a sperm sample that has been altered by us to carry some of our genetics. The resulting embryo is allowed to incubate no more than four months at the maximum and then is removed without any trauma to the physical body.

This is not a very widespread situation. More often than

not you will be given detailed communication through the subconscious that this is taking place so that you will not question or become traumatized when the fetus is removed. We are being reminded once again by our facilitators to stress to you that this is a co-created choice, and that this is not a usage of you as a laboratory animal. It is an agreement on the part of both of us that you will assist us in creating a joyous blending of our two species for the purpose of our own evolutionary leaps together.

Sometimes after these children are gestated (approximately 10-12 of your developmental months), you will be allowed to be brought to the incubation chamber and interact with these children for the purpose of giving them the love they need, which we are so far incapable of giving them. This is also for the purpose of our monitoring and researching your maternal responses. Though we cannot understand it, we know the definition of poignancy. All the demonstrations of emotion and affection are quite poignant between mother and child. It is understood to be a very joyous and profound experience. You are assisting in the birth of another race.

When this suddenly dawned on me, I felt good about it. It is not that there was any fear or regret.

Thank you. There are others on your planet who may not feel that way. If you encounter them, we would encourage you to share your feelings.

If a woman is without a partner, is there a situation where a fetus could be created?

It can come from a human donor. We call them donors, but those of you who are in fear may say it is "taken." We have vast sperm banks. Some of the sperm may be taken from those banks.

Even if you have a partner in your life, the child may not be of his donated sperm. It may or it may not be.

25

I remember seeing a six year-old child on a ship. She was with two people. She had scars on her face. I bent down to acknowledge her. It was very important for me to love this child. They said she had been sick. I said I didn't care, that I wanted to kiss her. I kissed all of the scars on her face. I felt a lot of love for her. Was she mine?

Your emotions will answer the question for you. Trust those emotions.

What happens to these hybrid children as they grow up? On Earth, children who are not given love experience some very traumatic emotional difficulties. In an environment where your species is unable to give children love, what happens to them?

We have surrogate caretakers who are taken daily to the children in order to give them love. Understand that the population of your planet is great. There is no shortage of loving females. Even some males provide love for these children.

Are these surrogates humans who are taken in the physical state?

Yes. You asked what happens to the children. Many of them do not reach maturity, which is why we are working so diligently to find the strain we will concentrate on. Many of these do not continue, and we are told to tell you that they live full lives while they exist. There is no regret, no sadness. They enjoy their time when they interact with you and receive your love and give you love in return.

So you are saying they die before reaching adulthood?

Yes. There are several who are surviving but retain a weak state; those are kept in specially created environments on a ship. The desire for the future is to create a planetary environment in which they can populate. We are not at that stage yet.

With our DNA as part of their genetics, they must be able to feel emotions to some degree. Therefore, are they happy in the environment you provide?

They radiate a calm, peaceful and strong spirituality that we would consider to be happy or content.

When you say that you consider them to be happy, you are evaluating that from a standpoint of no experience. Would someone such as Bashar evaluate their emotional state as happy?

Yes. We have other species who work with us frequently, such as Pleiadians. They evaluate it in the same way.

Do these children get the opportunity to bond with individuals?

Not one on one. That is not our way.

Is that not useful?

It is our understanding—whether we are in error or not—that your one-on-one bonding with parental units are sometimes (more often than not) dysfunctional.

It is my understanding that the Zetas have been collecting a lot of data on codependency and addictions. Are you familiar with this?

I am familiar with some of the units that are providing information. I do not have it all in depth.

Well, why all the curiosity in that area?

Our society was once severely dysfunctional and addictive. If we can understand dysfunction, we can understand how not to recreate it once we reestablish emotional connections. We seek to understand our past in order to move into the future.

27

Do you have any idea what the percentages are now on our planet of people who suffer from dysfunction?

It is very high. It is within the ninetieth percentile.

Are you saying that bonding in and of itself is a negative expression?

Not *all* bonding. It depends on the nature of the bonding.

It was the positive kind of bonding I was referring to that would be useful to the child in your environment.

My consciousness does not understand the idea of bonding one on one because to us, we are all one.

I am suggesting it is possible because of our emotional nature that without that kind of bonding, we would not have the will to survive to adulthood. That could be a possible reason why the children you have there do not grow to adulthood.

You have an idea on your planet called "kibbutz." This is not necessarily a one-on-one bonding, and yet the children are loved. We are certain that this is not a major role in their ceasing to function.

A lot of us experience our interactions with you as being quite frequent, and then all of a sudden there is no contact. Are the interactions really cyclical like that? What kinds of variables would account for this?

From our point of view, we never cease communication. Your perceived gaps in time are merely your way of orchestrating the timing. Do you understand what we mean?

So our own growth and development would then determine when we would have that experience?

Exactly. You perceive gaps between the experiences you are having on your quasi-physical or dream state level. To us, it is a constant interaction.

28

I have a line of questioning I would like to pursue. It has to do with the quality of the detainments [abductions] of children in the 1950s and 1960s. What effect has this had on them today? Is there a response on the part of the Zeta Reticuli in changing the quality or flavor of the detainments with the children of today?

We have not done anything differently in the quality of our detainments. The difference is in the state of the mass consciousness. In the 1950s of your time you were still allowing yourselves to feel vulnerable. You were still allowing yourselves the possibility of being victims more thoroughly than you are now. The children who were allowing themselves to be temporarily detained then were incarnate in order to play out that idea voluntarily. Through the decades, you are allowing yourself to come to terms with your own feelings of victimization and disempowerment. You are, as you move through the decades, allowing yourself a major transformational shift. What would you like further?

What we have noted in our observations is that there was a lot of psychological damage done to people being abducted — primarily due to the misunderstanding of the nature of the event. I can assume by your answer that the same damage is not being done today as it was then?

Children who are detained today really fall in line with the idea of conscious volunteering. There is less detainment today and much more volunteering. That reflects a species shift.

We will simply say again, thank you for allowing all of us to hold hands together and to make the quantum leap. Our gratitude is extended to you.

"...from so simple a beginning endless forms most beautiful and most wonderful have been, and are being, evolved."
— Charles Darwin, in the *Origin of Species*

3

Sexuality and Zeta Reticuli

> *"Sex was one of the symptoms expressing our dysfunction, and so we denied it along with the rampant emotionality that ran through our culture."* — Harone

In an attempt to understand the Zeta Reticuli psyche, one can examine their views on sex and sexuality. There is a high degree of clinical curiosity. It also seems there is an intense desire for experiential understanding that has so far eluded them.

The Zeta Reticuli have not yet understood the link between emotion and sexuality. Try as they might, they continue to examine the chemical nature of sexuality while struggling to understand how human emotions can be expressed through this chemistry. This desire for absolute understanding on their part drives them toward seeking an integration between biochemistry and emotion.

What follows is a conversation with Harone. Harone is a project leader for some of the genetic experiments. He has spent considerable time among humanoid beings from other races and uses his insights in an attempt to communicate to humans about the Zeta Reticuli purpose and intention.

* * *

Harone: We spoke earlier about the history of the Apexian system. A clear understanding of this history will allow you to understand how we evolved the way we did and why we know there are certain things that we need to reintegrate into our beings. Let us discuss our physiology and sexuality.

In our past, we vowed never again to allow passion in our lives in any area. So we began cloning out of our bodies all physiological reactions that could lead to an emotional response. We actually took out the physical, neurochemical reactions that produced emotions. We wanted to react in a completely balanced way to any kind of stimulus that we encountered. There was no longer any emotion or varied response.

We discovered that we had made a mistake. The cloning process we had developed to solve our original planetary problems resulted in weak cellular structures with no variance and no adaptability. We knew we needed to return to a process of biological procreation, which also meant a return to emotional responses. But our physical bodies were now totally incapable of either. We had no sexual organs. We had no physical differences between the sexes. If you were to look at our males and females standing next to each other, you would see no difference.

So when you are choosing a Zeta body for your life, it makes absolutely no difference whether it contains an XX (female) chromosome pair or an XY (male)?

Correct. There is no physical difference. There is no psychic difference either — no polarization of energies. This was because of our decision to remove all emotional reaction and to become one totally fused mind.

We decided that our individuality was not healthy. It was an individuality with a denial of the Whole. We then sought to become the Whole, and thus we denied the individuality.

32

Now we see that we have polarized even further, and we wish to bring it to center by incorporating individuality within our wholeness.

Are you in the process of trying to integrate this individuality by attempting to reincorporate sexuality?

Yes. We recognize it is a vital function for physical, biological beings. We feel that sexual behavior can help us experience emotion. We have seen civilizations on other worlds who are very integrated emotionally and still have sexual relations and procreate as a species. These qualities are desirable to us, and would serve our race well if we could incorporate them.

Do you express any physical affection for one another at the present time?

No. There is no reason to, or there hasn't been in the past. We believe we understand what you are asking. There is really no one-on-one interaction between us, but there is interaction as a group. What remains of any type of ceremonial behavior we might have is a merging with whoever is physically present at the time. We form a circle, hold hands, and merge with The One. When we commune in this way, we lose the focus of our day-to-day tasks and gain the focus of the Whole. So you could say it is a sensation of expanding and merging. We would assume it is the closest thing we have to sexual interaction or affection.

Do you feel any love for the others during these times?

I do not really understand what "love" is, but I do believe the correct response would be no. We resonate with an idea, not another individual.

Those on your planet place such an importance on the sexual act—an importance that goes beyond the need for procreation—that it makes us very curious. We see it is connected to emotions, but we are at a loss to understand it.

33

So what happened at the beginning when your race first denied its sexuality?

The energy was channeled into other areas, especially into our mentality. Not until generations upon generations later did we understand that this increased focus into our mental processes was narrowing our view of reality. We realized we could no longer see new ideas.

Whatever passion you had was removed from all physical and emotional aspects of your life and directed solely into your mental abilities?

Yes, so we could solve what we thought were our environmental and genetic problems. We assumed that we had become imbalanced because we had allowed our emotions and our passions to supersede our mentality.

Was there any thought that the denial of sex would lead to a higher spirituality?

We didn't look that far ahead. Primarily we saw that sex was one of the symptoms expressing our dysfunction, and so we denied it along with the rampant emotionality that ran through our culture. It was not until after the denial occurred that we began exploring spiritual connections with sexuality.

Who decided when a new body would be cloned, when life could begin for a new Zeta?

It was simply decided by the need within society for another participant. The authority does not come from one position or individual. It is a realization overall throughout the group mind that more are needed.

Now you are attempting to regain emotional response by cloning it back into your bodies?

Perhaps *splicing* it back in would be more correct.

Are you at the point yet where you are beginning to feel twinges of physical and emotional response?

We may be at the brink of beginning to feel, but right now even jumping into a fire would simply be a curiosity. We would feel no pain. The way we gauge our "feeling" is by how intrigued we are with an idea. If there is curiosity and a single-mindedness toward the discovery of an idea, then we know perhaps that road leads to the discovery of emotion.

When you realized this curiosity about sex, what did you do about it?

We knew we needed a gene pool that would allow us to reintegrate our emotions. We needed an existing genetic structure from which we could take the DNA and splice it back into our own, to reestablish the chemical reactions for us to feel emotions again.

Did you find one? If so, where?

Yes. Your Earth. Your planet has all the primary genetics from our previous history, and it's all in one place. It's perfect.

Please understand that we are not doing anything against anyone's will or wishes. You have invited us, whether you know it consciously or not. We have always assumed your subconscious was the voice of your conscious. Now that we have been communicating with you for awhile, we have learned that you do not always know what your subconscious says.

We have looked to humans whose subconscious minds have invited us in, and we did not realize that these invitations were sometimes not recognized by the conscious mind. We have also understood that the part of a being that makes it sentient — you call it a "soul" — can give permission for certain events to occur. There is no such thing as someone being preyed upon or being a victim. You will always draw to you

35

what you want or need to experience, because you are as curious as we are.

With this in mind, then, we have approached your planet and sought out individuals who have given their permission — whether on the conscious level or the soul level — to become participants in our experiments.

You have never performed an experiment without the agreement of the human being involved?

Correct. We cannot perceive those who do not completely agree. We literally cannot even *find* them physically because of the differences in our vibrations.

We have been watching you throughout most of your recorded history, because we understand that the development of your culture could possibly parallel ours in the past. However, our curiosity reached full force in your 1940s.

In the 1940s we saw that your civilization had gotten to the point of possessing the ability of total destruction, much like ours had earlier. We understood and recognized that you were at a threshold. You could go either way. You could annihilate yourselves or you could reach the unlimited potentials of consciousness. We saw that we could be of service to each other.

We started by gaining permission to view humans in sexual acts. This provided a storehouse of data that we do not yet know how to process. We have very basic conclusions that are not representative of all the data. No conclusions we reach are ever true across the board.

The next step was to obtain the assistance of humanoid races not of your Earth to engage in sexual encounters with humans. We viewed these experiences to see if an interaction with another species would change your sexual behavior. We are not yet able to interpret the data. You encounter an emotion at times that is like a wall to us. You call it fear. We cannot read beyond this fear, and so this has considerably slowed our data collection.

Harone, this is going to ruffle some feathers on Earth.

Please remember, this is *only* done with your agreement.

And we have also agreed not to remember these incidents?

Correct. There are some who *do* remember, but apparently they experience the emotions you call guilt or embarrassment.

That may be understandable. When does this kind of thing occur?

First of all, we will interact with you at night simply because our eyes cannot adapt to your sunlight; they are too sensitive. So let us say that you are sleeping in your bed. You suddenly become aware that there is a being standing next to you. A great many of you approach this idea with fear. *We have no intention of frightening you!* Think of it this way: If you were to meet a strange culture on your planet, perhaps you would unknowingly frighten them!

What was the next step in your experimentation?

It was for a Zeta to have a sexual interaction directly with an Earth human.

Allow me to explain that there are at this time three forms of Zeta consciousness interacting with your planet. First is the **straight Zeta**, which is a very high vibrational energy that cannot interact with you physically. These Zetas can appear to you only in quasi-physical states such as the dream state and other altered states of consciousness.

Category number two is **altered Zeta**, and this is the broadest category of Zeta Reticuli. The reason for the alteration is so that we can interact with you on a more physical level. The unaltered Zetas will interact with you for the purposes of learning through energy — through viewing, through

37

observation. Those who interact with you in any form of physicality will be of altered Zeta stock.

The third category is a **hybrid consciousness**, which is a combination of Earth human and altered Zeta. This hybrid consciousness is primarily unstable, although there are some strains who are able to communicate with you and who can physically interact with you during your encounters with our race.

I place myself within the category of altered Zeta. I am unique in that I have a very small percentage of Earth genetics. But I could not be in the hybrid category.

How is this alteration done?

There is a stepping down in vibrational frequency accomplished by placing a straight Zeta into an environment energetically and vibrationally charged, which will simulate a denser reality. It is like the immersion of a being into another environment to get them assimilated to a different density. The state of altered Zeta can be permanent or it may be only temporary. It is both a physical alteration and a psychological/psychic alteration. The consciousness will change as one is introduced into a new environment.

Is the hybrid category formed by taking Earth DNA and using it in a cloning process with an altered Zeta?

Correct. It will be done through various laboratory procedures in which human DNA is successfully bonded with altered Zeta DNA. One of the difficulties we have had in our experiments in creating hybrids has been trying to discover the correct environment for the altered Zetas before the bonding to the Earth's DNA occurs.

So why would an altered Zeta want to have sexual interactions with humans?

To play at the sexual encounter, to see if it triggers emotions in us.

You have said that your sexual organs were atrophied. How does this encounter occur then?

We can simulate organs. It is simply the solidification of energy into matter through the focus of thought. We cannot yet create any physical sensations through these simulations, though. We are not fertile with these simulated organs, either.

No children have been born on your planet yet that are the result of these experiments. They may have altered DNA, but they are not considered hybrid.

The issue we are working on now is the strengthening of the immune system of these children. They possess portions of the human immune system and portions of ours. We are finding a bit of difficulty in achieving a stable balance.

We are in the second stage of this development, and our projections are that stage three will begin in your 1990s. That stage will encompass a more integrated aspect of both species to allow for a greater number of hybrids to be created.

One experiment we conduct involves the impregnation of a human female. The child lives within the womb for three to four months and is then removed. The child could not live on Earth because of the differences in its vibrational frequency.

Another experiment is when a female is impregnated by seed that is primarily Terran [Earth] but with altered DNA structures. The child is altered in such a way as to become the next evolutionary step on your planet, but it can still survive on Earth.

What do you imagine that you're looking for emotionally?

In our understanding, imagination is based on emotion. Our imagination only spans what our mentality can create. We understand that we cannot become like you because of our evolutionary processes; but the ideal that we move toward is physical procreation and an expression of oneness through physical contact, not just through mental or spiritual contact.

We have heard that your females wish to learn once again how to nurture and love children, and they are viewing humans in order to learn this.

In our history, we created a separation between children and adults that grew very wide until we no longer knew how to reach out and cradle them in our arms. Often XX Zetas [females] are chosen to run the maternity section for our hybrids. This is with the thought that certain maternal instincts we once had might be reactivated. So far, there is no change in the feeling. That is why we are so honored by your agreement to help us remember how to nurture those children. Your civilization is teaching us love in a way that we have not experienced for millennia.

When we create fetuses of your race and ours, please do not think that we are callous or cold. These fetuses are the forefathers of a new race — a new race that is part of *both* of us. We cannot express to you what that means to us.

The only way we can measure the feeling would be through our level of curiosity — and there *is* a high level of curiosity with the creation of the hybrid babies. That is why in some of the work we do with your race, females and males are brought to give love to these infants. We understand that because they are part human, they need human tenderness and love. We are not capable of giving this to them, so we invite humans aboard for two purposes: to give love to these children, and to teach *us* about love.

So is it the decision of your race that you are incapable of feeling love solely because you don't have the right chemicals in your bodies?

That is the theory. This is also why we put organic implants in humans — not to control your behavior, but to absorb the neurochemicals in your brains that you secrete in response to

40

various emotions. We later process these chemicals in our laboratory. We are attempting alterations of *our* brains to simulate the chemical responses that you have in yours. This must be done gradually, however, in order to let our brains get used to the new secretions.

Do you recognize any spiritual nature to your being?

Yes.

Isn't there an understanding that simply because you are a spiritual being, you can love?

We understand that philosophical question, and through our analysis would have to answer yes. But knowing that answer is true has not yet allowed us to love.

So it is your premise that this breakthrough to love will come when you have been able to regain the chemical ability through the creation of a new physical body?

Yes. As we work with altered Zeta bodies, we are incorporating the simulated neurochemicals that we create in the labs from the data we collect from you. We then couple this with our observations of human behavior. The premise is that the combination of the neurochemical simulation and the observation of this behavior will trigger a chemical-emotional response in us.

Can't you simply decide to stop rejecting your emotions?

Our method of rejecting emotion is different from your psychological understanding of this. Out of our past desperation, instead of suppressing the emotion or drawing the emotion within, we rejected it completely. We also altered our brain structure so it would not output varying responses to external stimuli. We dropped emotion out of our physical bodies rather than suppressing it. We knew emotions could not *really* be suppressed psychologically, that they simply come out in a different way.

41

Is there any concept of self-love or self-appreciation?

Yes, but not as an individual — as part of the Whole.

Do you feel that as an individual you make any unique contribution to the Whole?

The only way I can answer is that there is one uniqueness you will find in my race: Various ideas create varying degrees of curiosity in various individuals. It is the one vestige of individuality that we possess, and it is what has allowed us to survive.

Do you love yourself for that unique contribution?

Please understand that I am affected by years of evolution. To me, the idea of loving myself or appreciating myself for this would be a waste of energy that can be channeled into the Whole.

Your civilization is very, very individualized, and you do not feel very connected to the Whole. We, on the other hand, are like a mass mind. We each have our own identity, but that identity is not what motivates us in our lives. The connection to the Whole motivates us, and we therefore receive all the nurturing and what you would call love through this connection. We bred out our emotions because we thought we did not need them. From our point of view, you are highly individualistic and highly emotional.

There seems to be so much difference between us that I still wonder why you're so interested in Earth.

For several reasons. You are approaching a point that we were at a very long time ago. We moved from this point to the creation of cataclysmic changes on our planet. You do not have to take that route. You have a choice, and this is the time for you to make that choice. It is also a perfect time for us to interact with you, because the chemical you are secreting will also simulate or parallel the chemical that we were secreting in the same circumstances.

You see, when we began our cloning process, we totally shunned our past. We have no records of what we were like prior to that time. We have no way of knowing, for example, our indigenous chemical make-up when we could still feel emotions. You are the closest we can find to what we may have been. We are attempting to heal our past. It's that simple.

There is an agreement between our species. You are teaching us about the love we supposedly have within us that we want to unlock, and how not to fear our own individuality. We are teaching you about your fears and how you can turn those fears into your strengths. Our relationship is a symbiotic one, for we are all part of the same Whole.

> *"...a species lives on if, and only if, it gives rise to other species — that is, if it changes. If not, it dies."*
>   — Howard Gruber, stating Darwin's Second
>   Theory of Evolution in *Darwin on Man*.

4

The Abduction Process

"Your base genetic structure in combination with your sociological evolution named you the prime candidate..."

— Harone

Some of the most common questions asked concerning the whole abduction phenomenon are also the most complex. People want to know how the process is actually carried out and whether it is actually a physical, energetic, or psychological experience. At this point in time, the tip of the iceberg has not even been approached. The interactions with the Zeta Reticuli occur on physical levels, dream-state levels, quasi-physical levels, and probably any level we can imagine.

Before we can really begin transforming our relationship with the Zeta Reticuli, it will help us to have more solid information about their reality and how they view us. By examining some in-depth technical information about how they perceive their human interactions, we can gain significant insight into their world. Let us not forget that this is the perfect opportunity to observe the observers!

The following conversation may shed light on some of these technical questions. Harone speaks candidly about his reality and how he views the agreements between the Zeta Reticuli and humans. He also answers pointed questions about

45

several of the most common concerns individuals have about the abduction phenomenon. Though the information is by no means complete, we take one more step toward understanding the enigmatic race of the Zeta Reticuli.

*   *   *

I'd like to open this conversation with a question. What is the nature of the agreement or permission perceived by the Zeta Reticuli that allows them to abduct, detain, and experiment with humans?

Harone: The nature is simple. We view your collective soul as being a part of ours and therefore by that unification, permission is granted.

How is that perceived on your part?

Simply because we are able to carry it out. Permission is there. If we were not able to carry it out, then there would have been no permission.

But initially you must have perceived something before you first started carrying this out. There must have been some type of logic that allowed you to carry this out in the first place.

Our logic may not be accepted by humans with their rational minds, perhaps. However, because we possess the ability of time travel, we are aware of probabilities. We are aware of probabilities for Earth. We also know our past. We know that Earth has a very strong probability of heading in the same direction that we did. Therefore, as a member of the universal races, it is our responsibility and also our gift to assist planets in their evolutionary steps. When we became aware of your planet, there was an instant recognition that we could give you something and you could give us something.

I am trying to get this into perspective for people who view this situation as definitely not one of agreement and consent.

46

There is no way for us to change their minds. You see, this aspect of agreement is part of the evolutionary steps you are taking on your planet. When individuals continue to deny that they have agreed to any given thing in their reality, it halts their evolution.

Okay. This level of agreement doesn't take place with the individual, true? Meaning that many individuals who are part of your activities have said, "No. Don't do this."

Part of them have. The greater part of them that is linked into the Whole has said yes.

What does it sound like? What does it look like when you communicate with that part?

It is an allowance. It is as if a gift is given to us.

When we discuss these matters among ourselves, an agreement must be written on a piece of paper. Or it must be spoken verbally. If someone agrees to do something with me, I have heard them verbally.

How many times have you experienced nonverbal agreement? You experience nonverbal agreement nearly every moment you exist. It is just more subtle, so you do not understand that it occurs. Every time you have an interaction with a person you are experiencing a nonverbal agreement. Therefore if you draw someone into your realm of being — your reality — there is automatically an agreement. It cannot be otherwise.

You see, for humans the idea of agreement is that it is separate from existence. This means the agreement is something that stands out from the flow of your life to prove to yourself that you can have a certain experience. We perceive *flow* as agreements — reality as agreements. The fact that we are here — that we are with you — *is* agreement. You place cause before effect, however, cause actually *equals* effect.

47

I think what we don't have an agreement about is the defini-tion of what an agreement is.

These agreements do not conform to human definitions. They cannot, because your definition of agreement (as you have said) is either oral or written. Even when oral or writ-ten agreements are created, there are loopholes to protect yourself. It is not freely given. These agreements go beyond physicality. They exist within the very fundamental nature of your being—your soul.

We view agreement as also an act of the will. It is a decision.

A decision of the *ego.* You separate the ego from the other portions of yourself.

In our definition, that would be the nature of agreement. It is a separate act.

It is the nature of *your type of agreement*, but you are evolv-ing. You are changing. There are agreements surpassing the ego's viewpoint of agreements that are much more powerful in your lives.

So the decisions of the individual personality carry very little weight, if any, for the Zeta Reticuli?

With your words, it seems to us that many of you will not *allow* yourselves to understand what we say. You somehow feel we insult your persona. We do not.

My current questioning is formed by what I perceive much of the population thinks and feels.

There may be several types of agreements created. For ex-ample:

1. Some other extraterrestrial species who feel they own you could give the "ownership papers" to us. Therefore you would be our property. That is an illustration. That would be

48

a concrete agreement you would understand. But that is not the case.

2. Your species could take a mass vote: "All those in favor of interacting with the Zeta Reticuli, please raise your hands." This is also not in effect because you have not yet allowed yourselves to accept even our existence. Thus that type of agreement is not applicable either.

The only applicable agreement at this time is the agreement on the most basic level, which is the agreement of our collective souls together. From that point of view there is no difference between our races.

Your theorists on your planet have much difficulty in understanding our motives because they are not willing to challenge their intellect or their fear of the unknown. Once you ponder our motives, you *must* take into account the nature of your own soul. If you do not, a great portion of the equation is missing.

I personally follow you very well. But what I understand may not help others who need to benefit from this information.

We cannot put it any other way, for we state the truth as we know it. We certainly do not wish to tell you that your "ownership papers" have been given to us. Although that might comfort many on your planet (so they would have someone to blame), it is not the truth.

That is an idea in accord with our mass consciousness — we can be owned, because we have owned others.

Exactly. That may bother people. But beneath that sense of bother, there might be for some a great sense of relief because they can then understand the dynamic. You have had thousands of years of slavery. Our relationship with you is a relationship of equality, and *that* is the lesson that needs to be learned.

49

In our ideas of agreement, there must be an inquiry and an answer. That is where some of the confusion is. We as individuals who make up a species do not ever recall hearing the question. Therefore as far as we are concerned, consent cannot have been given because the question has not been asked.

Consent is given on the *level* that the experience takes place. For the most part we do not interact with you in your waking, day-to-day reality. We interact with you during states of altered consciousness. *During those states of altered consciousness you very openly give agreements.*

Even now on your planet you have allowed yourselves to believe that your day-to-day reality is the only true reality and the other states of consciousness are subrealities. As you have learned from your metaphysical studies, this is not so. Actually, *the day-to-day reality is more the dream than any other.* Permission is given on the reality in which you exist *all the time,* not the dream reality you find yourselves in when you are awake during your daytime.

Is there an actual inquiry done on those other levels?

There is only an inquiry in the sense that the vibration is put out and those who wish to be a part will signal us.

Would it be to your benefit for those of us involved to receive the inquiry and answer it in this reality?

In the long run it would be beneficial; however, for a period of time it would throw a great amount of confusion into our work as well as yours. We would not get accurate readings if we were to listen to your waking voice more than your "real reality" voice. Also, the fear this would bring up would permeate your day-to-day lives in such a way that there would be distraction and confusion from the things you feel you need to be doing on your planet. Right now our interaction is existing in the only balanced way it can. However, the eventual plan is for there to be a waking recognition of our interactions;

this will gradually seep into the waking consciousness of your planet at a rate that the mass consciousness can accept. To do it any faster than that would be a shock to the system.

So in your eyes we appear to have multiple personalities? It seems like you have to be somewhat careful with us.

That term, we understand, has negative connotations in your society. We do not view you as negative or positive. But we do view you as fragmented, for you do not have an awareness of what occurs on other levels of your own consciousness.

So our identities in our waking state are fragmented. Are they fragmented on our other levels of consciousness?

Your other levels of consciousness are more integrated. You are in the process now of integrating those other states (such as the subconscious) into the conscious so that you will become more integrated beings. Therefore you will know more of what is occurring on other levels of reality rather than just this subreality.

Back to the agreement being given on other levels: There are numerous cases where people are experiencing trauma in the waking state. What is your reaction when they experience that?

Simply the idea that the information — the understanding — has broken through the barrier between the unconscious and the conscious, and that this is the way that particular individual has chosen it — through trauma. You can say that their revelations, their understandings, are actually felt throughout the mass grouping of your consciousnesses; eventually, that type of traumatic understanding does serve the whole. It is like breaking through a plastic barrier and releasing the pressure so that everyone may feel the release.

This we neither condone nor prevent you from experiencing. Your mass consciousness will choose how to process our experiences with you in the way that you need to. We have no control over that; we choose to have none.

51

How do the Zeta Reticuli initially choose the abductees? How do they find the person in their location? How does your authority, your Network, make that decision?

There are several answers to this question. The most common answer would be that those from our mass mind will choose to live lives as Earth humans. As we go into those lifetimes we will go with the thought, the knowledge, the motivation that we are going into the lifetime for the purpose of interacting – as a human – with us, the Zeta Reticuli. We encounter again a barrier for people on your planet who do not embrace the idea of a soul or who wish to look at life as finite. Those who wish to continue with this point of view will have their intellectual processes stymied very strongly.

As individuals from our civilization come into existence on your planet, they carry with them a signature vibration that is coded within our computers. You may consider it a homing mechanism. At certain points in the development of the physical being the homing mechanism will be triggered. It will register on our mass computers and we will be able to find the person through the registration of that homing mechanism. This is very easy.

Also, periodically we will generate a beam of electromagnetic energy with the request for contact encoded within it. The vibration within this beam speaks to the overall reality (not your conscious subreality) and asks for volunteers for part of our work. Those who respond with a return vibration are noted and catalogued. They are found when it is appropriate.

Back to the homing method: How is the original signature decided on? Is it implanted or catalogued first?

We catalogue their personal vibratory signature. The vibrational signature has a set of instructions (so to speak), and at a certain developmental stage (which is decided before the incarnation) there will be a burst of signal returned into the ethers and we will home in on it.

But how do you initially get that information?

Every living being has a signature vibration. Even inorganic matter has a signature vibration.

But how do you initially program the computer to listen for that signature? How do you make the decision? Does the soul get coded in your ship so it can later be called up?

Yes. To put it in primitive terms, a fingerprint is taken to be used later.

The signal goes out, the computer finds the fingerprint, and then you start the relationship with the person?

Exactly.

Are there other ways that you take the fingerprint from people who are not of your mass mind?

The second example we gave you was when we generate random electromagnetic beams looking for volunteers. When a volunteer "raises his or her hand" we catalogue that signature vibration, which can be done at a distance. We note the position in the space/time continuum. We evaluate their developmental age, their circumstances, and we pay them a visit when the timing is appropriate. Sometimes we interact with someone who has volunteered and then realize that their genetic structure is not adequate for what we need. Then we ask them to be surrogate mothers for the hybrids, or emotional support systems for other abductees. The services they can provide are infinite. They do not have to be direct "abductees."

You mentioned only souls from your mass mind. Is that method used with other souls?

Yes. There are souls from other civilizations — any that you can think of, including Earth — who choose interaction before incarnation, so we catalog them from their energy state.

Is there some sort of conversation before the incarnation? Are these matters discussed?

Not in the way you understand discussion. Do not limit your sense of communication. Understand that there are beings of Zeta origin who exist in very high vibrational realities approaching nonphysicality. They are the bridges to communicate with these beings who are about to incarnate.

Okay. Let's say that back at "Computer Central" a particular vibratory frequency has been activated. The computer signals someone that you can visit one of us. What is the next step?

The next step is to insert ourselves first in what you would consider to be the dream reality of the person. This allows them to begin forming a relationship with us, in an archetypal sense. This will be carried out several times until the unconscious structure of the person becomes acclimated to our energy. Then there will be more of a direct communication that can take many forms.

We have skipped a part of the scenario. I want to know how the Zeta Reticuli get here when they first receive the signal to begin the communication.

We are already here.

You are in local space?

Yes. We are in interdimensional space that requires simply a flip of a switch in order to enter your reality and time continuum. We are not limited by time and space.

Is it a physical ship that is housing the decision makers?

It is not that clear-cut. Obviously the ships in which the abductees are taken are indeed physical. When you talk about interdimensional realities, the terms "physical" and "non-physical" become moot points. If something is not in your dimension, you call it nonphysical. However, it can be very physical in that other dimension; it just does not share physical space with you.

The first time a person experiences contact, where do the Zeta Reticuli come from? How did they get there?

They are generally from a ship that has been interacting in the interdimensional space in the vicinity of your planet.

Is there any traveling back and forth to Zeta Reticuli?

No. We are entirely self-sufficient.

So I suspect that many of the Zetas in the vicinity have never been to Zeta Reticuli?

Correct.

But the term "Zeta Reticuli" still applies?

It is what *you* call us.

Do you have a name for yourselves?

One People.

So we have a crew sitting on a ship. A signal comes in. The command to make contact comes in on computers or communication devices. Give me a typical scenario of a first contact, before a familiarity sets in with that person.

From our point of view, there is no familiarity. Let us give you an example. Understand that we will simplify greatly so you will understand it. (This is not meant as an insult.)

When a signal is sent, the computer translates it, matches its signature vibration with the catalogue of signature vibrations, and automatically sets the ship's course for the location in space/time of the signal's origin. We simply do our job and do not worry about the driving.

55

Now again we simplify. Bear with us. We then go into the transportation device and are automatically transported to the place in space/time where the person exists. There is no doubt who it is when we get there. Many things are taken care of before we arrive.

What you are describing is some type of massive computer system.

It is linked with our mass mind.

So it is not something that is entirely separate from your mass mind. Is it linked with any computers or mass minds back on Zeta Reticuli?

Most of this operation is not generated from the system you call Zeta Reticuli. There are remnant groups still living there, but it is mostly generated from our vast network of ships, for we are living (as you would call it) in space. There is no reason for us to return to our planet.

Do you intend to return to any planet?

Not in the form we are in, no. There is no reason to.

Do your brains actually form part of that vast computer?

Yes. Through harmonics, not through wire connections.

Is there a central processing area?

There are multiple processing areas. A very crude example would be that you can generate a harmonic frequency within your head. As long as you generate this harmonic frequency, you are linked into the mass whole. You can sever the harmonic frequency at will and thus sever your connection to the whole. There is no reason for us to do this. However, we will do it in case of "capture" or "accidents," as in the case of crashed disks. We will deliberately sever ourselves from the computer.

Why sever yourself?

56

For example, if one of your limbs were to die and became totally useless — a leg for example — and was still connected to your body, it would actually be more difficult to drag it around. It would be much easier to sever the connection with that leg, and, as you say, lighten the load.

Do these crews spend most of their lives on that ship?

Yes. There is no reason to leave it.

When the signal comes in to go and communicate with someone, what does a member of that crew see, hear, and think?

We are signaled by the massive computer when it is time to conduct an interaction. We cannot tell you it is bells ringing or an announcement over the loudspeaker. It is not. It is a telepathic signal knowingness that it is time.

But it has to come through as hard data somewhere. It has to be in the ship's navigation system.

We are downloaded all the information we need into our brains.

But you do have onboard computers, correct? Or are they more of a reference device to allow greater accessibility to the mass mind?

You would consider the main brain system of the computer to be organic. From there are extensions of inorganic hardware with which we can interface.

Reports from people who have been on ships describe lots of controls, though — screens, lights, etc. Does anything show up on a screen?

Some of the interactions recounted on your planet are embellishments by the subconscious in order to make sense of the situation. Some are examples of cruder technology that other of our races possess. Thus there is not an across-the-board description of technology on our ships.

57

Okay. So the ship gets the data on this person and it goes through space and time to find them. When it comes to that area, does it stop and hover over the house? Does it signal the occupants that it is there?

There is no need to signal *us* that we are approaching the target, for we are ready for the interaction. It is instantaneous. There is no "finding."

So the ship translocates itself to the homing signal.

Yes.

Does it occur at the proper time, or does the crew choose when to begin the communication?

The crews make no conscious decisions. The mass mind makes all decisions according to data available and will transport exactly at the time and space that is necessary.

So if a person is due to be abducted that night but they are awake and using the bathroom, does the crew wait for the person to finish? Do they simply appear when the person has gone back to sleep?

There will simply be an appearance when the time is right. They will automatically appear when the person is in the appropriate state. Even if we surprise the person in the bathroom, it is meant to be that way. It is not calculated by the crew. The mass-mind computer calculates it all.

Interesting. That is a rather overwhelming thought to us...

Because of your individualistic nature. You feel as if you have given your power to something else.

Yes. It feels like the individual has no power.

But yet there is no difference between our reality and yours. You simply create the illusion that you are *not* moving with the flow, that you can strain against the flow and make con-

58

scious decisions against the flow. But every decision you make is *in* the flow. It *is* the decision you *need* to make. There is no difference between our reality and yours. It is only a difference in perception.

Since you are time travelers, why don't the Zeta Reticuli travel back into their own time to get what they need?

Because it is our understanding that our past does not possess what we need. We do not possess in our past an integrated version of the genetics of the galactic family of which we are both a part. Your planet does.

Genetically "integrated"?

Yes. More than we were.

But yet you have all the genetic variance in your own past. You can integrate them as you choose to.

But our past does not possess the thousands of years of evolution genetically that you have.

So it is the experiential value of the genetics that you don't have?

Exactly. Experience affects genetics in a very strong way. For example, a primate learns how to use a specific tool; the use of this tool is picked up gradually, primate by primate until, through birth, it has become a natural instinct. This is how experience can affect genetics.

The past of the Zeta Reticuli does not possess the same experiential processes as the human race does. The genetics that you possess is a more advanced version of our base genetics. If we were to get genetic material from our past, we would be getting only a more primitive version of our own genetics.

Aren't there any other societies out there who have what we have?

There are some societies who were tested; however, they possessed the base genetics in ratios different from yours. Your base genetic structure in combination with your sociological evolution named you the prime candidate.

How do the Zeta Reticuli actually bring humans aboard their craft during an abduction?

Some of this experience is generated by our mass-mind energetic field before we even arrive. It will place the human in an altered state of consciousness. When we arrive, we generally immobilize the human through what some of you call paralysis. This is only so that humans do not hurt themselves physically.

The transport can occur in several different ways. One is by altering the molecular vibration from matter to energy; then a shift in the space continuum brings them onto our ship. They resolidify into matter once again. Another form of transport reverses the polarity of the body in relation to the Earth's gravitational field; we can thus guide you physically into an awaiting ship as if we were pulling a balloon on a string. The accounts of humans passing through walls and doors is simply an altering of the molecular vibration of the human enough for it to become less dense and pass through solid objects. It is really a very simple procedure. Our intent is to do it during a state of unconsciousness in the human so as not to frighten them unduly. However, some retain memory of this transport.

Have you ever tried asking a person in the waking state to come aboard the ship?

We do have some contacts who are aware and volunteer in the conscious state. However, we cannot communicate with you in the conscious state. It is like you have a dog whistle that only dogs can hear. Our states of reality are so different that your conscious mind cannot hear us when we "blow the whistle." Therefore you generally can hear us only in altered states of consciousness. However, sometimes when your brain-wave patterns fluctuate, you can perceive us very briefly while you are awake.

What about the probes that are inserted? Describe the various ones you use and their purposes.

The most common is a probe of an organic nature that is inserted into the brain. It can be inserted through the sinus cavity, the ear, or the eye. Its purpose is to collect and catalog neurochemical data. This is of great assistance to us in our genetic understanding, for it assists us in giving the hybrids a balanced neurochemical make-up. These probes are inserted and left within the human for a given amount of time and then taken out for the data to be catalogued. It is not a painful thing, where the human would know it is there, for though it is organic, it is composed of a very condensed plasmic light energy. It can be dissolved at will if there is a chance of detection.

There is another probe that many have been concerned about and frightened of. This is to probe the anal region of humans and is done for several reasons. It is our understanding that humans would like to be made as comfortable as possible, and we understand that sometimes in traumatic experiences there is a loss of bowel function. This process cleans out the colon area so that does not occur. The fecal matter also provides us with data about the human digestive system. Also, in males we can extract secretions from the prostate gland through this probe.

People frequently have reported painful irritations in areas where your devices have touched them. Can you talk about this?

These irritations are not in any way directly related to the physical insertion of these probes. It is actually more related to the idea of memory loss. For instance, if someone has a nosebleed, it is indicative of the memory wanting to break through. The physical body generates the trauma it has been exposed to. It recreates the trauma to trigger the memory recollection. This is a common psychological reaction in humans, we have found. This is also applicable for all repressed traumatic experiences that humans have throughout childhood. These spontaneous painful experiences are merely your own healthy psychological processes attempting to reveal information to you.

Do the devices you touch and probe humans with have any organic or inorganic substances on them? Can a human react allergically to them?

Our environments are totally sterile. There would be no chance of this.

So rashes or sores that would come from being poked and prodded would fall under the explanation you just gave us?

Yes. We would say that there are some groups that are much more clumsy in their experiments, and sometimes they may indirectly cause discomfort to the human. But we would say that in most cases — 80% of the time — it is simply a way for the body to establish a recollection of the memory by triggering the physical traumatic response.

How is paralysis generated during the examination or insertion of probes?

Simply by exposing certain areas of the brain to an electrical charge that causes the paralysis in the person. It is entirely harmless and actually serves the body in a positive way — like rejuvenation.

How is it applied?

Sometimes the electrical frequency is generated by our mass-mind computer before we arrive. Sometimes we do this through a long, slender, needlelike apparatus.

Does this penetrate the brain?

No. It feels as though it does, but that is simply the electrical current.

What is the significance of the emotional visions that abductees have during an encounter? For instance, some people have seen a nuclear holocaust. They've seen their own death, or other visions that evoke a lot of emotion.

It has been mistakenly thought that we are giving humans prophetic visions. This is not the case. After insertion of probes into the brain, it becomes essential for us to gather the neurochemical data by providing stimuli for the human to react to that will allow their brains to secrete the chemicals we can later study. Such traumatic visions like nuclear holocaust and death are merely holographic scenarios created within the brains of the humans—however real they may seem—in order for them to react and secrete the chemical we wish to study.

Let us express something: Though this process may seem like a cruel form of torture, *it is our understanding that we are generating in humans a way for them to face their deepest fears, which will actually allow them a transcendence to another state of evolution.* We do not perceive that we are intruders in the night from outside of your world. We perceive that we are visitors from your *internal* world who are facilitating a coevolution for both of our species.

Memory loss and missing time...does the ego protect against trauma also?

There are times when we will deliberately induce memory loss in the humans that we interact with. This will be done simply because in our evaluation of their psychological state it will be obvious that the conscious memory of such an experience will not be of service to the human at that time. However, it is very common for us *not* to induce memory loss. The natural psychological functions will take over in the human that will either create a screen memory or block out

63

the experience totally. Understand that these experiences will take place for the most part in altered states of consciousness. Because the experience is not conscious, it is dreamlike for the person and therefore much easier for the defense mechanisms to block memory systems.

How are the Zeta Reticuli able to use time travel in their experiments and the breeding program?

We have attempted an answer to this question in the past, and we understand that it is very difficult to comprehend with linear thought. However, if you imagine a single line and a point above that line, we exist from the point and you exist in the line. From the point we can enter any area on the line. We can go into the future; we can go into the past. From our position within that point, we discovered your race. That is when we decided to begin observation and interaction. From that point we simultaneously projected ourselves into nearly every segment of the time line in which you exist.

So as I speak to you now from a certain point in our experiments, there are others existing simultaneously in other time frames. It is our understanding that the heaviest interaction we are having is between the years 1935 to approximately 2020 — give or take 5 to 10 years. So we are not limited by *your* progression of time.

Is that where some of the confusion comes from? Because we have little choice but to use our linear model of time to interpret our experiences?

Yes. Our reality is nonlinear in the most extreme sense. Your reality is very linear in the most extreme sense. It would be like apples and oranges.

Therefore much of our relationship with you is misinterpreted because of our two different types of reality?

Exactly.

64

That is why what we think happened is not necessarily what you think happened?

Exactly.

In view of allowing us to understand the experience more, you mentioned yourselves as visitors from the inside. Could you expound on that to assist us in understanding our relationship with you more?

Again, we must speak about the metaphysics of the universe. Reality is a creation from within. Though you can look in your telescopes and see stars and distant galaxies, you are really only looking at the walls of the outermost portions of yourself. Everything you see is a reflection of *you*. Everything you experience is a reflection of an aspect of *you*. We are visitors who come in the night because you have not yet been able to openly accept us in the daylight. We are still a frightening experience and thought for you. We can exist with you right now only on those archetypal, subconscious levels within you. You are still creating us in your altered states of reality; yet you argue about our existence in your conscious state of reality. But your altered state knows the truth. **We are visitors from within**. We have lives and existences separate from you, yes. But we are *within* your consciousness as you are within ours.

So are we visitors to you from inside of you?

Yes. You are facilitating our evolution from within us as well. You allow us to face *our* deepest fears — fears we are only now beginning to understand we possess. Coevolution.

Humans have within their power the ability to bring us out from the depths of the shadows of the night and into the daylight of your waking, conscious selves. It is your choice. But it will require you to confront head on the unknown and that which you fear. If you are ready, you will find that your fear is but an illusion. But you will never know unless you attempt it.

5

Hybrids and their Creation

"...We are picking up where your forefathers have left off. We are facilitating another species leap for the human race — for both your benefit and ours." — Harone

---

Something is going on. The data from contemporary abductees can at times be quite haunting. Some speak of the removal of sperm and ova. Others speak of being pregnant and suddenly having the pregnancy terminated with no after-indications of the previous pregnancy. Some of the more bizarre stories speak of genetic laboratories where half-human infants struggle for survival. One thing is clear: These stories reflect a consistency in detail and emotional flavor from all over the United States, Europe, Japan, South America, Australia, and other countries on Earth.

If this isn't an actual physical phenomenon, then something is happening on a species level within the collective psyche of humankind. The phenomenon itself cannot be ignored any longer. It is time to plunge headlong into the depths of those black and shiny eyes.

In this chapter, a conversation with Harone (the project leader for some genetic projects) is presented. He addresses some of the most common questions asked about the creation of hybrids and the purpose for their apparent desperation to create a new race. There are still many more things to discover, but perhaps his information can trigger a deeper level of understanding for individuals who grapple with these questions daily.

* * *

In regard to your genetic work, let us talk about the etheric and physical aspects of your activities.

Harone: To us, both etheric and physical aspects are equally important. Upon your world, you understand only half of the process of creation because you are looking only in the physical realms. So we will attempt to give you information to show you how we conduct this work on both the etheric and the physical levels.

First we will begin with the etheric levels. Your scientists have discovered atoms and the aspects that make up atoms — protons, electrons, neutrons. Your science is only now exploring even smaller particles. There are still smaller levels of reality from the electron level that are gaining a lot of attention. The etheric work that we do is done on a meta-atomic level. This level surpasses the level you can now see with your most finely tuned instruments. It is a level that exists outside of the physical dimension, although you simultaneously exist on this level. The primary means for manipulation on this level can be considered light plasmic in nature. Light plasma is induced in various areas to create specific codings, or a language. The physical matter adjacent to this nonphysical state forms itself according to the light plasmic language that is set up.

When we do our genetic work in the creation of hybrids, we first begin on the most basic of levels, which to us is the meta-atomic level. We will create a template around which physical life will eventually form itself. What you call your genetic structure — chromosomes, DNA, RNA — represents some of the smallest genetic codes you can read right now. But there is a world beyond that. That is the world in which we begin.

We begin, first of all, by harnessing the template that exists for all forms of life in the reality we share with you. This template is a triadic structure that represents one polarity, its opposite, and the integration or the joining of the two. Life forms the way it does because of this template, which exists in the reality we share with you. We begin with this triadic template.

Within the energy dynamic of this template we then insert plasmic light energy with the language encoded into it at the most basic levels. It is difficult to describe exactly what this language "says," because it is a language that does not exist in physical reality. Its components eventually instruct physical matter how to create body structures. The language first affects the nonphysical, and then the physical realms. Work on the etheric level can be likened to building blocks. From the most basic level, the plasmic light language instructs the physical matter to arrange itself according to the these etheric templates. We always start with the triadic template. We have been working on many different strains of hybrid beings to find the most resilient ones, so we alter the light plasmic language attached to the triadic template in order to find the most perfect body structure that can serve us.

Before you talk about the physical work, can you bridge the two? Can you talk about how your work in the etheric connects with your work in the physical?

Physicality is always connected to nonphysicality, so what is done in nonphysicality will always affect the physical realms. There may be, in your terms, a time lag between the nonphysical work and the physical manifestation, but that is only because of the idea of growth in an exponential sense from nonphysicality into physicality. You see, matter is matter because it has compressed itself enough from the energetic state to form a densified field. When the template is given enough light plasmic energy, it becomes compressed and enters the physical realm. This is the bridge.

Thank you. Now can you talk about the physical aspects of your work?

Your scientists may consider that the physical aspects are much more easily manipulated. But once we have what you would consider to be a fetus, we then can monitor and direct its biochemical development so it will have the right mixtures and proportions of chemicals needed to develop the type of being we would like to create.

The physical genetic work continues throughout the life of the hybrid simply because we have not perfected the strain. We must continue to achieve the perfection that we seek. This is done through experiments in neurochemicals, adrenal chemicals, and basic chemical function in the body. It is also achieved through directing various light and sound frequencies on the developing fetus that will give it the signature vibration it needs in order to develop according to our plans. On all levels, then, the genetic work is done. The etheric level is the most basic, but yet is instrumental in the forming of the physical level.

How are the hybrid fetuses taken from the human host mother?

As you know, the fetuses are either implanted or are naturally conceived and later worked on genetically. Anywhere from one to four months (usually no later) they need to be taken out of the human embryonic environment for the next stage of work to be done on them. The methodology of removal would depend, of course, on the individual Zeta group taking the fetuses. We do have our different ways. But the most common way would be through a method that requires the "surgeon" to vibrationally alter the molecular structure of the host mother so that she becomes less dense. The surgeon is then able to insert his hands into the womb and remove the child with no scars or blood. It is, in your terms, a method of psychic surgery.

Other forms would be a more sophisticated method of removal through the vaginal tract. There is no pain, and also there are no scars left to ever show there was a pregnancy. This has baffled doctors on your planet. Those are the two primary methods of fetus removal.

Are any surgically removed in which incisions are left?

Only the less adept of researchers will remove fetuses through surgery. But that is very, very uncommon. Even if it is removed through a surgical manner, there will not be stitches. The skin will be closed up with lasers. If there are any detectable traces, they will be very fine.

Any other methods?

There is one other method that is used infrequently. It has to do with the isolation of the fetus into a different vibrational continuum. The space of this vibrational continuum is altered so that one moment the fetus is in the womb and the next in our laboratory. This method is frequently used for diagnostic checks and sometimes the fetus is reinserted into the female host.

How are human males used in the hybrid experiments?

The role of the human male, as you know, is different from the female because males cannot be hosts for embryos. But they provide vital genetic samples (such as sperm) that are altered in our laboratories and used for further fertilization. Also, there is a substance extracted from the prostate gland that is very useful to us in understanding how to reestablish our reproductive capabilities. This research is not in any way complete, but we are recognizing the value of some of the substances extracted from human males.

.Human males are also used as support systems for the females. Frequently (not all the time) when the primary sub-

71

ject is female, the secondary subject is a male spouse. The male spouse will provide emotional support for the female not only on the physical waking level, but also during encounters with us in altered states of consciousness. We have found that having the male as a support is of significant value.

Both male and female neurochemical data differ, and our working with the males is helping us to understand the differences between male and female. This will assist us in the creation of stable hybrid beings.

Tell us something about the strains of hybrids, both the successful and unsuccessful.

As you may be aware, as we speak to you in your present time continuum we have not achieved the stable hybrid strain that we are seeking. But we have made much progress. The unstable strains primarily have dysfunctional immune systems, which resulted from the differences in vibrational reality between Earth plane and the realms we exist within. They still need immune systems — different types of immune systems — and we have not had sufficient data or understanding to provide them with these immune systems. So frequently they would appear to be quite sickly and would not live long.

There was one strain that would live for approximately three to five developmental years, and then the body would consistently begin to deteriorate. This specific strain, we discovered, was not able to process nutrients that we thought their bodies were absorbing. So in a sense you could say that their demise was caused by starvation. We were not aware that this was occurring. Once the degeneration began, it continued until the entire body was lost. This occurred at a very rapid rate.

The difficulties we have had include the processing of toxins and the taking in of nourishment through the skin. We have not been able to create a skin covering that is a strong combination of our species and yours. This is something we still work on.

We have had problems with the pituitary hormones and growth regulation. We have had hybrids whose bodies grew much quicker than was healthy for the body. We have had hybrid strains who would grow very slowly from child to adult, and a form of deterioration would occur because of this slow growth. It has not been an easy creation process, but vital data was collected along the way.

When you speak of immune-system difficulties, what exactly do you mean? I suspect in your laboratory conditions you don't have many biological organisms floating around.

True. When we speak of immune-system difficulties in our realities, we are talking about the body's ability to screen out harmful cosmic radiation. On our level of existence, that is how the immune system functions. You, as part of a planetary ecosystem, have a natural ability to use ultraviolet light and to adapt yourselves to the specific radiation you are exposed to from your sun. This is due to millions of years of development. These hybrids do not have millions of years to adapt and so it is trial and error, as you say.

Some of the hybrid strains that were unsuccessful displayed symptoms of radiation sickness—loss of hair, inability to process nourishment, loss of appetite, and general weakness and malaise.

What about the successful strains?

We have had some success in creating rudimentary reproductive tracts in some of the hybrid beings. So far, as we speak to you in present time, only one of these hybrids has actually been able to conceive and give birth to a live child. There have been some stillbirths—a great many, actually. But we consider the successes to far outweigh the failures because our work on the creation of reproductive tracts has been quite successful.

We have not yet been successful in creating an emotional expression system that we would consider to be perfect, though we have had success with some of the neurochemical data we have received from you, which has allowed some hybrids to experience a small range of emotion. This emotion would primarily be joy and enthusiasm. Some have experienced laughter and the emotion of compassion.

What about negative emotions?

Not yet.

Loneliness? They are somewhat a one-of-a-kind being.

We would say the emotion of loneliness would transfer into the emotion of compassion, for a given hybrid would not feel loneliness for itself but compassion toward another. They have not yet developed the ability to feel loneliness for the self, because that is still an idea of individuality.

What would the source of laughter have been?

The source was through interactions with humans who have been teaching hybrid beings human behavior — play, laughter. This is done with the humans in an altered state of consciousness. It is not consistent, but it has been known to occur.

What can you tell us about the Essassani species — the hybrid species?

This is where it gets tricky. Let us give you some background. The species Essassani exists in contemporary time that we share with you now as members of the Association of Worlds. They are known as the civilization that has evolved from our hybrid work. However, *in our real time* they have not been created yet. So the key to their creation is not yet totally understood to us; otherwise we would already have created them. But we know (and they tell us) that as we continue with what we are doing, we will achieve their creation.

74

It is through the marriage of you and us. That is really all the clues they will give us.

You personally have been in the physical presence of an Essassani. What was that like? Was it a bit confusing?

It was curious, but I wouldn't say confusing. It was a source of great curiosity. In your terms, we would have liked to have gotten the Essassani under a microscope, but we all understand that is not part of the agreement, for that would be like taking a short cut. This is a process that we must *achieve*. None of them would volunteer.

Have you asked?

Yes.

If they did, wouldn't it be like the continual weaving of the tapestry?

Yes, and it is not illogical to think that perhaps sometime in the future one of them *will* volunteer. It will be their way of ensuring their own creation. But at least for now, none have volunteered. We are speculating that right now your civilization and our civilization need each other. The extent of this need is not understood yet by either of us, but as soon as we no longer need each other perhaps that will be when one of the Essassani will volunteer and we will have the key we need to create them.

We know that the Zeta Reticuli are taking our DNA. But are they doing anything to us?

The wording of the question would suggest that you have nothing to do with this, and we would certainly deny that. It is a co-creation between our two races. But yes, we are facilitating something within you that is the culmination of a very ancient agreement.

The genetic work on your planet with your species began from a more primitive form of life over a million of your years ago. This genetic project was not consistently undertaken, but left to simmer for thousands of years at a time. The last phase of the in-depth genetic work done on your planet was just before your "missing link" developmental period. At that time, it was not the Zeta Reticuli doing that work. In this time that you call the present we are picking up where your forefathers have left off. We are facilitating another species leap for the human race — for both your benefit and ours. We recognize you to be a very valuable force in the galactic family, and we understand that your development will be beneficial to all. We also understand that you, as souls, have agreed to this millions of years ago.

We know that there are scientists and researchers on your planet involved in the empirical understanding of the "abduction" phenomenon who would wish to discount the key element — the soul. There is a part of you on an inner or mass-conscious level that knows exactly what is going on. We say to you that this part cannot be discounted, for that is like using an equation and leaving out a missing piece.

The common question is, what is it we are doing? We spoke about the light-plasmic language that we use on meta-atomic levels. This is one of the ways we are helping you to achieve a species leap. When you partake in experiments with us, yes, you give us something. But we also give you something. That something is more codes, more activation on the light-plasmic language level. This is occurring with literally thousands of people on your planet. There will be a critical mass reached, and when this happens, the species leap will occur in force.

What type of code? Can you explain the ideas that are represented there?

The ideas are primarily representative of vision, meaning that your vision has been limited since your inception. You have seen yourself as a being whose country or family was only as far as you could see. You are now (in the last forty years) achieving a global vision so that you are not just, in your terms, Americans but citizens of a global civilization.

Primarily, the code we are triggering within you is the recognition of yourselves as part of a *galactic ecosystem*, a working piece of the whole. It is a code that will allow you to expand your vision, and with this expansion you will see that some of the structures you have created for the last several thousand years can no longer serve you, and you must adapt your structures to your new vision.

When we say vision, we are also talking about the metaphysical idea that you create your reality. Your limited vision has created a limited potential. Now it is time for the unlocking of the unlimited potential, and that potential will equal the expansiveness of your vision. We see the work that we do with you as *galactic evolution*, and since you've experienced only species planetary evolution, it is a new arena for you. But there are guides, there are facilitators who have been there before who assist you.

Are you doing anything like mixing our own DNA globally?

We are not mixing your racial codes. But there are various programmings inserted within you by your forefathers that developed into different codings in different races. For instance, your ancient story of the Tower of Babel is a symbolic representation of your forefathers' inserting contradictory codes into various groups of people on your planet in order to keep you diversified and separate.

We can now be considered to be symbolically taking those codes back and reprogramming you with a code that is made up of all races, so that each and every one of you have a code representative of *all peoples* on your planet. You will begin to speak the same language symbolically.

Do you mean in our thinking and feeling?

Yes.

What about a linguistic language?

This will facilitate the creation of a global language more quickly. But it will be something *you* will develop and learn through education. Our work will facilitate the means, the desire and the motivation to do so.

What are the various ways that the Zeta Reticuli create hybrids using our genetic material?

We were talking about the triadic template, so we will start with that. After the triadic template, we take codes from ourselves that we consider to be of value. We have already learned how to isolate which codes are what qualities, so that is already known. (When we say "codes," we speak of vibration—vibrational structures.) We begin with the triadic template and then locate the codes or the qualities locked within a vibrational signature that we wish to retain in the creation of the hybrid race.

For instance, the preponderance toward unity rather than diversity would represent one of our valued codes. Also, the idea of being a group mind is valued. It will be expanded upon later and lessened in intensity using your DNA.

Then we would take the qualities of humans that we feel are valuable and (speaking symbolically) wrap them around our own codes. This will create an energy field that will begin an integration of both codes. For instance, the qualities of yours we find valuable would be your love of individuality. When mixed with our code of mass mind, we theorize it will be a very stable balance. We also use your drive for reproduction, for perpetuating the species. We also value your love of emotion, and that is wrapped around our code for absence of emotion. Again, we theorize that this will produce a stable balance in the emotional bodies of the hybrids.

This creates the condensed energy field that forms into matter, so that will be the template for the developing hybrid.

After that it is simply biochemical adjustment in combination with vibrational adjustment.

What do these various strains of hybrids look like?

The most successful strains so far have had very light, translucent skin; large heads with more developed frontal lobes; either hairless, white or silvery hair; eye structures that can perceive wavelengths of light beyond your visible spectrum; small nose; small mouth, but we are still working on the creation of a digestive tract; a very simplified excretory tract; reproductive organs similar to yours; approximately four to five feet in height; either four fingers and a thumb, three fingers and a thumb, or three fingers and another appendage that we would not call a thumb; very sensitive hearing but without a large external appearance of an ear like you; and a heightened sense of smell and taste.

Some of the unsuccessful strains were much smaller and much more fragile. Some of them had craniums too large to be supported by their bodies, and as they grew they would frequently experience what you call a broken neck or deformed neck vertebrae supporting a head disproportionate to the body.

Were they assisted with prosthetics?

Yes. But when we understood that the vertebrae were unable to support the head, we knew we would have to start over and that the prosthetics were only a temporary solution.

Do any of these hybrids have tear ducts?

Some of our more recent strains do because we understand the human structure does, and therefore we are attempting an emulation. But they are not in total use at this time except in cases of foreign matter in the eye. They serve a cleansing function, but we have not yet made the link with tear ducts and emotion.

Have you ever kept a human fetus unaltered?

79

Yes.

Can you tell us why you did it, and what the results were?

When we have kept human fetuses unaltered, they have provided us with some of the most valuable data about human beings that we have ever received. We will point out that the souls of the fetuses were ones from our community who chose to incarnate as human to have us observe the development of the body. So it is not something that we have "stolen" from you. Do you understand?

Were they fetuses taken from a human female? Or was it ones you grew yourselves?

They were ones we grew ourselves, taken from human donors. They were human, although we did have to make vibration alterations in order for them to survive in our vibrational environment. Other than that, there were no genetic codes altered. This was because we wished to observe the natural developmental process of a child. It provided us with fascinating data as simple as cranial size in proportion to body and the ability of bone structures to hold certain degrees of weight. It also provided us with data about balance and symmetry in the human body. It did not necessarily provide us with as much neurochemical data simply because in our environment the beings were not exposed to a lot of emotional stimuli. It was mostly to record the development of various body structures such as the reproductive system, adrenal system, cardio systems, circulatory systems, digestive systems, etc.

Did these humans display a need to be nurtured emotionally?

Yes. We allowed human females who have volunteered to nurture the children.

What age do they live to?

They will indeed live to adulthood and once they stop growing, they will not age. So the body will continue until the soul decides that it wishes another experience or until it is agreed upon that we are finished with the experiments.

Why is it that the Zeta Reticuli sometimes present babies to humans and then watch their reactions?

This has a multifold purpose. One is that we recognize the need humans and semihuman hybrids have for nurturing. We have had many hybrids die because of lack of attention and warmth. It has taken us many tries to learn the connection between this emotional bonding and survival.

When we made this connection we began asking volunteers to come and nurture these children. They nurture the children to sustain the life of the hybrid child. Also, it allows us to monitor the neurochemical secretions that occur during such a bonding exercise — the neurochemicals of both the mother and the child — so that we can perhaps have emotions stimulated in us. We can perhaps learn how to nurture as we once did so very long ago. So far, these presentations have not triggered emotion in us, but at the same time we recognize their value.

This nurturing of hybrids on the part of human females occurs much more frequently than many realize. It is more common than is the actual abduction occurrence.

Where does the encounter take place?

Within our laboratories perhaps 75% of the time; 20% of the time within the room that the female is sleeping or resting; and 5% in various places such as lounges or in a neutral location. It could be in a simulated-dream reality creation that the human female can accept, such as a hospital room or her childhood home.

Is this always done in the physical?

81

Sometimes in the physical, sometimes in the etheric. Etheric interactions are more common, perhaps 55%. This is because to the female they are less threatening. Physical presentations occur 45% of the time. Of the 45%, 40% occur in an altered state of consciousness. Only 5% occur consciously.

Do you get different results when the women are in different states of consciousness?

Yes. When the woman is totally conscious, the energy she emits emotionally is very intense for us — even a positive emotion of love and nurturance. We do not utilize the physical presentations very frequently for that reason. It is not only for our protection, but also because the hybrid child is half Zeta. Therefore, we theorize, the emotional emanation from the human female in physical form may be as intense for the child as it is for a Zeta.

What do the children experience?

They experience a very archetypal idea. Obviously we cannot communicate in the same way with the children at the time of the nurturance, but what we are able to gather is that they feel a sense of connection with life. You must remember that all of the hybrid beings we work with are Zeta souls (or Earth souls) choosing this experience. So they are not crying out in anguish. But yet the interactions with the human females allow them to feel connected to life and give them the strength of survival in order that we may carry out the experiments. You may also call it love. Since we do not know love, we cannot tell you if this is the emotion. But it is logical to assume that it is.

Do the hybrids experience any discomfort or fear? Unsureness about being part of the experiments?

Not generally. As has been stated, all the hybrids are souls who have deliberately chosen to enter this experience. So from that understanding, there is no fear or sense of victimization. There is no self-pity. They are joyously partaking of this experiment. The only discomfort they may feel is when one of their physical vehicles is beginning to cease functioning. They will feel the life flow ebb from them. This may be a confusing experience for them, but other than that, there is no sense of cruelty. There is no fear.

Do the hybrids ever take part in abductions later on?

Yes. Some of the hybrids who have lived to adolescence or adulthood work with us in the detainment of humans. In the research on your planet, this can account for the many different types of beings encountered by abductees. (We use the term "abductees" only because it is *your* term, not ours.)

It is theorized that the usage of hybrids during abductions will give the abductee a sense of comradeship—that there is someone there who shares at least part of their reality. It is also theorized that perhaps a trigger of emotion will occur on the part of the hybrid during the interaction with the human.

We have one more thing to say. We speak to you now from your time continuum that is roughly the transition point between 1990 and 1991 as you count time. It is our understanding that within the next ten of your years the hybrid experiments will be nearly complete. We do not know how this will occur, for it is only a theoretical projection. But you can hasten the pace of this work by understanding that there are no victims and that we have all chosen interaction in this way together.

The hybrids are symbolic of a marriage between our species and represent the future of both of our races. They represent the best of both of us. They represent the potential of the human soul.

83

> *"Any woman who gives birth today could well be the new Mitochondrial Eve, the mother of the new species..."*
> — Yatri from *Unknown Man:*
> *The Mysterious Birth of a New Species*

6

Changing the
Abduction Experience

"If you don't like the experience, you can change it. This understanding is central to the entire abduction situation.
— Germane

We've examined the abduction experience from the point of view of the Zeta Reticuli. We've looked at their history, beliefs, and reality. The next step will require us to synthesize all that we've learned and begin making the experience work *for* us. We cannot force these visitors to change, since we really are not sure what we are confronting. Therefore, what remains is the most logical solution: change ourselves. If we can change our perception of the phenomenon, perhaps we can alter the experience itself.

In this chapter, Germane first gives techniques that can help us alter or stop the experience. But he carries it further than that. As the session unfolds he presents a new viewpoint — one that requires us to take full responsibility for our actions and our reality. Are we ready to release once and for all our identities as victims?

* * *

Germane: We are going to talk about changing the abduction experience. This is the key to the transformation of this entire situation on your planet. Changing the abduction experience would be done in two different ways. One would be using certain techniques and the other would be by changing perception.

Learning to use certain techniques to change the abduction experience will assist you in changing your perception as well. As you change your perception, the experience itself must change.

We are going to talk about some techniques that individuals can use either when they are in the middle of an abduction experience or when they feel one coming on.

The Zeta Reticuli are not aware (for the most part) that you are able to understand enough about the experience to place yourself out of their reach. This information may be quite a surprise to them. Of course, this is part of their learning experience as well as yours.

First, we are going to start with the idea of pain. Many individuals may wake up in the middle of an abduction experiencing pain. Many have asked how they can change the experience of pain into something that is less traumatic — perhaps into a sense of neutrality. When some of the extraterrestrial beings are doing things to you that are physically painful (putting probes in you or examining you), they are aware of the concept of pain but are not necessarily in touch with the actual understanding of what pain is. Frequently they will place their hands on your forehead or the top of your head to stimulate areas of your brain to desensitize you to pain. The pain messages will thus not be received by your nerves. This will provide a soothing sense for the person who is undergoing the abduction experience.

86

What about the other end — the humans? When an individual is in the midst of this, what can you do to alleviate your own pain? The first thing to do if you are experiencing pain during an abduction experience is to create in your mind a very intense *electrical blue energy field* around your body. This is going to accomplish several things. First, the Zeta Reticuli are going to become aware of this blue electrical field. They are going to know something is up; they are going to realize that you have a certain sense of empowerment. So they will react to you differently. Then you will react to them differently. You change the cycle.

Also, the blue energy field that is placed around your body when you are experiencing pain will serve as an energetic desensitization whereby the vibrational frequency of your body is raised enough that your sensation of pain will seem more distant. This will allow you to have a further sense of empowerment that in and of itself will change the abduction experience.

Truly, if abductees do only *one* thing to empower themselves during an abduction experience, the abduction experience itself *must* change. If we were to say that there is a law at work here, that is it. What the abductee does will dictate the nature of the abduction experience. This experience is both an internal and an external one. It is external because these are real beings separate from you. It is internal because it directly reflects a dynamic that is occurring within you. When you change one thing, you change the entire experience.

That technique was given to help alleviate pain. Let us go a step further and give a technique for individuals who want to *stop* the abduction experience at midpoint. Let us say you are lying on the table and you become aware of this experience. You decide you want to stop right then. There are several things that can be done depending on the individual and their conviction.

The first thing an individual can do is proclaim from a sense of empowerment (rather than from fear or from a hope that the technique may work): "I do not need this experience in the form that it is occurring. I desire to change this communication." If the person has control of their verbal facilities, they can shout it. They can think it. Or they can feel it emotionally. The stronger it is proclaimed in whatever fashion, the more impact it will have.

The abduction experience really works in a very clear way with the idea that you are the creators of your reality. On your Earth you are not necessarily aware that when you think something, it manifests, because there are many things between the original thought and the manifestation. The abduction experience is more direct. It plays on your beliefs about yourself and your world. Therefore, if you believe you can be a victim, if you believe that somehow your world is being controlled — any of those types of beliefs — they will be played out and reflected back to you during the abduction experience. So changing the experience means changing those beliefs and proclaiming a new belief that you would like to express.

Many may think that this is quite a simplistic way to change the experience, but it is not. Those of you reading this material who have worked with clients through regression therapy will find (or may already have found) that as the client is beginning to become empowered, the abduction experience changes. It *must*. This is an absolute guarantee.

The first idea, then, is to make a proclamation. The second suggestion for changing the abduction experience is useful when you are unable to react verbally or in a way that requires thought, as some of the Zeta Reticuli will temporarily deaden the thought or speech centers. This suggestion is on a more primal level and requires the person who wants to end the abduction experience to emit a harmonic vibration. If you can do it through the vocal chords, do it that way. Or you can center the energy behind your third-eye area or the throat area and push it out. Remember, thought is vibration. Just because you cannot verbalize something audibly, you can still create a harmonic tone that can be felt by sensitive individuals in the vicinity of your expression.

The question then is, what is the correct harmonic tone? Each individual has his or her own correct harmonic tone. It will be different for everyone, so we cannot tell you on the musical scale which tone is right for you. It represents *your* signature vibration. When you allow yourself to express it spontaneously and with conviction, you will *automatically* express your signature vibration tone. If you are doing it verbally, the louder the tone, the more effective it will be. Do it with conviction.

This creates a vibrational ripple through the reality that you share with the Zeta Reticuli at that moment. The vibration can be likened to the shattering of glass. You are introducing a new vibration of *your* empowerment (because this is your signature vibration) into this reality, which will shatter that reality just like glass. It must be done out of a sense of empowerment and identity rather than out of fear and desperation. Fear will not have enough impact in the reality to shatter it.

When an individual uses this technique, after they emit the vibration, one of two things may happen: They will either be back in their third-dimensional reality or they will change the reality sufficiently so that whatever was occurring will change, and the beings they are interacting with will change as well. Therefore, the experience will be stepped up from that of examiner/examinee to an equal, co-created interaction.

You can practice this in your day-to-day life if you wish. But it needs to be practiced when you are having an emotional focus — most notably a negative emotional focus. If you are fearful, anxious or stressed you will feel a breaking point. At that point, emit the tone. If you practice it in your day-to-day reality, you allow yourself to be more familiar and comfortable with the process so that during an abduction experience you can do it without thinking about the technique. It will just come naturally.

Many of you may also be aware that when you are extremely happy (emotionally focused in the positive), you want to sing with joy. This is the same idea. When you have an emotional focus, you can channel that energy into a harmonic vibration that can significantly alter your reality. This technique, you will find, is quite powerful.

You mentioned stopping the abduction experience. But one of the reason the person is having it is because they've agreed to have it. Why stop it?

The stopping of the experience is only temporary. What is occurring is an evolutionary leap for the Zetas and the humans. The agreements will thus change. When the person realizes that they can be of service in a different way, *they will change their agreements.* That is part of the entire paradigm that is being shifted as well. It will be less of an unequal exchange and more of an equal co-creation. When we speak of stopping the abduction experience midstride, we are talking about stopping that particular encounter so that the person can go back to center and then reevaluate their own sense of power and identity. Should they choose to reenter the abduction experience, they will do it in an entirely different way. This will be the new paradigm that is introduced. This is going to be the inherent force of change in the entire abduction experience.

When I am in a fearful situation in this reality, sometimes it is hard to have the presence of mind to do what I know I need to do. When I am in that extremely fearful situation, how do I remember to do this?

Start with less fearful situations. Let us say you are driving down the road and you almost hit a dog. Adrenalin is rushing. Pull over to the side of the road. You are in a conscious state of mind at this point, so do it then. Start with more benign experiences and work your way up to the more intense ones. That way you will train yourself. It will become habit. You will be very surprised and pleased at how effective this technique is for allowing you to come back to center.

And it doesn't have to be verbal?

It doesn't have to be, though if you are able to do it verbally that is the optimum scenario.

What about the idea of synchronizing ourselves with the cycle of the Earth, which is about 7.5 cycles per second? In that way you can achieve a much greater sense of power than otherwise. I have heard that this might work.

That is a similar technique to what we've just spoken about concerning harmonics. This vibration is a signature vibration for Earth. You are part of a planet and have your own identity as well. If you were aware of the signature vibration of Earth, you could use that. We sense it would not be as profound as your own personal vibration, but it can be used.

Let us introduce another idea. This one may be quite frightening for many. Many may have a lot of resistance toward it. Let us say that you are in bed and aware that an abduction experience is coming. You are aware that they are taking you out into the ship and you feel helpless. What do you do? If you can allow yourself to do this, it will also switch the paradigm very quickly.

Stop for a moment internally. Get yourself centered. You will be able to do this because in times of intense fear, the energy is so focused that you can actually find a stillness within. It is possible to do this. When you get to that center, *allow yourself to give consent.* Communicate to the beings that you will voluntarily go with them. You are going to shock the heck out of them, especially if they have been interacting with you before and are used to your fighting them. This is going to alter the abduction experience for you. It *has* to, because

91

you are the empowering individual in this circumstance. You are calling the shots. You are changing the experience.

In this way you will open up a channel of communication between you and them. They will allow themselves to open up more freely and communicate with you on a much more intimate level so that you will be able to understand why it is occurring and perhaps even voluntarily give them data they are seeking. This will help them learn how to interact with humans in a much gentler way.

You will find that if you volunteer, not only will your experience change but you will feel more empowered as well. They will feel much more comfortable in communicating with you without all of the devices and methods they devise to get you in their ship. You start changing the paradigm. You change the experience because this is an archetypal, internal, extremely important experience for the human species.

This seems to me to be the most logical thing to do. This would be the best thing to shift it.

You know, when you are at the doctor's office and you are getting a shot, if you tense your muscles it only hurts more. *Anything that you resist persists.* In allowance you will find it is not as bad as you thought it was because you've given up that resistance. Now you can perhaps see the value that this experience can have. It is *not* an "us versus them" situation. It is two species at the opposite ends of the spectrum desperately trying to incorporate the values of the other, the genetics of the other, and open up lines of communication. That is really what it is all about.

With some of the more negative experiences — the ones with the beings who are more focused in the negative and are not concerned with the joint species transformation — the techniques we've outlined will be of significant value, especially the harmonic-resonance technique. From the entity's point of view, they wouldn't know what hit them. To them, *you will suddenly disappear.* We are not addressing here so

92

much the intensely negative abduction experiences, because they are only a small percentage of the abduction experiences on your planet. It is not the focus of this discussion, at least for now.

One of the major questions I have has to do with how little I allow myself consciously to be aware of this. It must be so frightening that I allow little awareness in. I've only gotten as far as being able to feel the energy present, so I sleep with the light on. If I allowed this to be more of a conscious experience, that alone would shift it, correct?

Yes!

But that thought is frightening. I just don't want to wake up with them staring at me. I would rather have it happen in the daytime. The biggest part of the fear is that they come at night. We have so many fears built up about things that happen in the night.

The nature of their communication with you would make it unusual (but not impossible) for it to occur during the day. Part of this is because it is easier to take you when you are already in an altered state. They can manipulate your memory much easier as well. That is a very obvious reason.

Another reason has to do more with the archetypal nature of the human consciousness — the darkness, the nighttime. That darkness is where you have to face the things that are terrifying to you.

The subconscious rules at night. That is when we are active on a subconscious level.

Yes. They must interact with you on the levels that represent the greater reality. For instance, your daytime reality is the most limited reality that you possess. Your subconscious reality and the realities in the altered states are more unlimited and represent more of your true nature. Humans

93

manifest these experiences mostly at night because the sub-conscious is equated with the night.

This situation represents humankind facing its deepest fears—fears of evolution, fears of change, fears of death or annihilation, fears of infiltration and control. These inherent, deep archetypal fears within the human being are coming from the levels of the subconscious and the unconscious and from the darkness within. You are manifesting these encounters according to the rules of the unconscious and the subconscious—the night, the shadowy realms, the realms between waking and sleeping, the realms in which you "are out of control." That is why it occurs. The more you can allow yourself to become comfortable with the realms of the darkness (darkness does not mean negative)—the realms of the subconscious, the archetypal fears—the less you are going to fear and dread the experience. When you say you are afraid you will wake up and find them staring at you, you are really only saying that you are afraid of staring into your counterpart that exists in the darkness. It always comes back to the self.

From the point of view of a species looking at you from a bird's-eye view, the human race right now is on the brink of an extremely powerful change—a change that will be more important than any change that you've made since you've made the leap to Homo sapiens. It is that powerful. *When a species is making a leap in evolution, the old part fears annihilation.* When it looks ahead, all it sees is darkness, because you haven't yet created the new species. So making that leap into the darkness is very frightening for many people. But the Terran species on your planet has made many leaps and managed to survive. Your level of sentience now is higher than it ever has been. This can work for or against you. It can work against you in the sense that all of the fears coming up may block you from taking a leap. But it can work for you because you can recognize how valuable and powerful that change is.

The Zeta Reticuli are paralleling you in terms of their own species leap. Theirs is different, for they are in a different

94

vibrational plane. But you are mirror images for each other and that is why you have attracted each other. What you do together will profoundly affect your galactic family. You will be creating a new species together. This is the way that evolution and creation continues and perpetuates in the universe. It is the first time you've experienced it, so you are a little unsure.

Once you no longer need to create them to come in the night, this entire situation is going to look very, very different. That will also be the time when you are able to look directly at yourself in the mirror through your own eyes into your own soul *and not fear what is within.*

Could someone request these experiences to happen in the daytime?

They have occurred for people during the daytime. However, in terms of the Zetas' ability, it is harder for them to come in the daytime because it is more difficult for them to access you and create the abduction experience if your brain waves are in beta state. If you are in alpha or theta state, it is easier.

But it is nothing for them to put you into that state.

Correct. But the experiences a human has in the beta state — awake and conscious — means that you are ensconced in the physical reality, and this reality is overwhelming for them.

Our conscious reality is too much for them?

Yes. They *can* do it, but your reality is very chaotic to them. They like order. Chaos is something they are not used to or comfortable in dealing with. To them, individuality is chaos. It is easier for them to get you when you are more merged with the One.

Isn't that why so many people have been shielded by the Zetas with those emotional shields — because they are so uncomfortable with our presence?

Yes. It is as uncomfortable for them as it is for you. For them it is like getting hit with a tidal wave of emotion. It is a physical sensation to them, a physical energy that hits them. If you were a Zeta and got hit with a similar wave of emotional energy, you would experience extreme nausea, loss of equilibrium, and your sense of breath and connection to the planet would be altered. They are certainly not having a party! As you and the Zeta Reticuli make a shift in your methodology of encountering each other, it will be less uncomfortable for both of you to make that communication.

Knowing those things helps make it a less frightening experience for me.

Each individual will also come up with their own different methodologies — whether they change the perception or change the technique. We wish to stress that *no one* is "sentenced" to interaction with the Zeta Reticuli without their agreement. If you don't like the experience, you can change it. This understanding is central to the entire abduction situation. The only reason you are calling the situation an abduction is because you've not yet taken your power and have not realized it is an agreement that you've already made.

We do need to start using a different language. The word "abduction" implies victimhood.

Exactly.

I've been thinking about that. What could we call it? My friends? My visitors? We need to change it to a positive connotation. The language must change.

Absolutely. That is a very important point. Changing your language will help you change your perceptions of the ex-

perience. Here are some suggestions: You could call yourself a guest, a visitor, an interacter, a communicator, an interface. Each of you can come up with your own term. Yes, the
language will need to change to reflect the change in your own
empowerment. That will significantly change the perceptions
of the experience. They are not abductors and you are not abductees. You are not being abducted; you have been *invited.*
You are a *guest.* Remember your manners when you visit your
friends!

If you were voluntarily going to a friend's house, your friend
would not grab you, throw you on a table and shove things up
your nose. When you walk in the door, they would say,
"Wouldn't it be fun if we could both learn something from
this interaction? Would you volunteer to give us a skin
sample?" If you said no, it would be respected. But you are
not even aware that you *can* say no, except out of fear. And
they don't understand the language of fear.

*If we've made this agreement, it must be exciting or interest-
ing to us on some level or we wouldn't have agreed. I would love
to have an interaction where they said, "Wouldn't it be fun if we
took a skin sample?" I could then say, "Yes! And I want you to
tell me all about your findings." Could we have that kind of exchange with them?*

Absolutely! They would love that type of exchange. They
don't think you are interested because of the way you react.
You may find that they would be willing to give you things —
but not for the purpose of proof that you had the experiences.
It would only be for the purpose of your excitement. They
want to share with you! If you asked *them* to get on the table
so you could look at their skin under the microscope, they
would say yes! *No one has ever asked them.*

*They may not have even conceived of this themselves — the
idea of changing the relationship like this.*

97

This is the reason why we are speaking to you rather than Harone. Harone is still in the paradigm. He cannot see it from outside. As you introduce these new concepts, their relationship with you is going to change.

And they will respond to those offers?

They will respond. From the higher picture, this is part of the plan. It is not meant to keep going the way it has been going. If both species are going to shift, your relationship with each other must shift first. One of you has to make the first step. They are making steps in their own way. But you can make your steps also. Perhaps using some of the information we've shared with you will enable you to make those steps. The idea of being angry and not being willing to let go of that anger at them will *not* change the experience.

You would remain a victim.

Exactly.

I feel a new way of thinking about this. Is this enough to begin shifting the experience?

Yes, certainly.

So the more I think about this and the more excitement I can generate about having an equal exchange with them, the more it will change the experience. But will it help it to happen?

It may not help it to happen the way you expect, but it will help it to happen in a way or a dynamic that will be exciting to you rather than frightening. The encounters may still be on the unconscious or dream-state level, but the *quality* of those encounters will shift. It may not become a conscious experience, but you will be able to see the effects of these changes in your consciousness in your conscious reality—for instance, when you don't feel you need to sleep with the light on anymore.

Or maybe I will move through some other fears in my reality as well.

Yes. They are issues of empowerment. Though they are connected to the abduction experience, they are also connected to other aspects of your life. Your *life* will change as well.

So I won't be as afraid to move into the dark areas of my life, whatever those issues are.

Exactly.

Let me reinterpret the desire for having the light on. On one level it is because I am afraid. On a deeper level it is because I want to see what is going on. I want to meet them face to face. With the light on, I am going to see them really clearly.

But they have got to want to see *you* just as much. In their own way, they are frightened of humans because of what you represent.

When they are in our presence, do they experience some type of fear?

Yes, but the emotion of fear is different for them than it is for you. They are very detached from it, but they know it is something they don't prefer. So they avoid it or attempt to control it so that they don't ever have to face it. As for you, you've been given all the tools you need to change the experience.

I just want it to be different—fun and exciting. If you really look at how this plays out in the whole evolutionary scheme, it is really an honor to be part of this.

Exactly! When enough people on your planet shift in this belief, the entire situation that they are co-creating with you is going to change. That is when you are going to see the major species leap occur. You are going to shock them, surprise

99

them, and allow them to become (in whatever way they can)
extremely excited. It is then that the sharing truly begins.

7

Behind the Walls

"For two days I had the feeling that I was being watched from some unobserved point. After two days I retired for the night only to be awakened in a sleep state to find a small craft situated outside my window..." — Leigh Washington

The visitor phenomenon seems to reveal more of itself at each turn in the road. Exactly how far have these encounters permeated into our society on Earth? Are there any areas we have not explored that perhaps hold a key piece of the puzzle to make the picture more complete?

A very articulate and intelligent gentleman wrote to us in early 1991 with some unusual yet fascinating stories regarding the alien contacts he and those around him have been having. What sets these contacts apart from any others we have researched is the fact that these stories come from behind the walls of a prison.

"Leigh Washington" (not his real name) is an inmate at a correctional facility in Michigan. During his years of incarceration, Leigh has been having repeated contacts since the late 1970s. The letters we have received from Leigh have all been extremely clear, balanced, and at times, slightly skeptical. Leigh has an open mind and a willingness to delve beyond the obvious. As his stories began to unfold, it became obvious that there was another area of the UFO phenomenon that had been overlooked. In Leigh's words...

> As odd and unusual as this might sound, I have had experiences with alien beings *while* being incarcerated...I use the words "odd" and "unusual" because most would assume that inmates are a worthless lot, given mostly to life's darker side. Sadly, such may be thought by many but this is not altogether true.
>
> I realize that being an inmate creates in the minds of most certain images and ideas that are not too positive. Let me assure you that even though I am in prison (and have been for 16 years), I have worked extremely hard to regain my oneness with the Whole, or All That Is. Where ignorance and blindness dwelt, awareness now resides. This awareness has put me in touch with much...
>
> I have felt for some time now that we — inmates in this particular facility — have been and are being watched. Speaking in generalities, I suspect that places such as these — where fear and blindness are prevalent — are prime areas for observation and even experimentation. I state this with a certain amount of doubt only because I lack definite credibility for my feelings. I suspect more than I can prove!

In all of Leigh's letters he plays the calm observer. Never has there been any indication of paranoia or grandiose claims. He often questions his own observations. That is what gives his information the eerie sense of reality we have come to recognize in his communications. What follows is the first account he gave to us of one of his experiences.

> For two days I had the feeling that I was being watched from some unobserved point. After two days of feeling this I retired for the night only to be awakened in a sleep state to find a small craft situated out my room (cell) window. Two aliens were standing near the vehicle while another was walking toward my window. As the alien

neared I had a definite impression it was me that it was interested in.

In the alien's hand was what appeared to be a long rod-shaped instrument (something like a wand) which I *knew* would emit a white beam when turned on. At my window, the alien aimed the rod at me. Just as the beam shot toward me I dashed to another part of my room. The beam missed. However, my movement brought me into a corner of my room which I could not easily move out of. [I was] trapped; the alien aimed the rod at the location of my third eye [between the brows] and fired. The beam struck. Immediately I was receiving information that I could not understand. My mind was full of symbols or maybe a language that was beyond my ability to grasp. After a short time the alien left and I woke up to recall most of the experience.

Any who have read UFO literature will recognize some of the familiar themes: A long, rod-shaped instrument; being hit with a beam of light in the forehead; and the transmission of symbols or information at a rapid rate. But what is really shocking is the implication of these experiences.

In the previous chapters we have presented information about some of the experiments that extraterrestrial groups have been conducting here on Earth. Let us put ourselves in the place of these extraterrestrials for a moment. If we came to Earth to conduct research and experiments, what is one of the conditions we would wish to maintain during our tests? *A controlled environment.* What kind of controlled environments are already intact on Earth? *Prisons.* If we were seeking data on intense emotional reactions (or seeking the biochemicals from them), where could we find humans in controlled environments experiencing intense emotions? *Behind the walls of a prison.*

We've already seen from the information presented previously (as well as from classic UFO abduction literature) that ETs often present scenarios to the abductees in order to observe their reactions. Leigh tells an interesting story along these lines...

> [One night] a group of us were taken for what I believe was some sort of reaction testing. This was the first time I can recall this kind of testing. In the morning I could only remember four of my fellow inmates who were involved. I was one of these four. I talked to two of the three and only one could remember. This was Kevin. He said that he was sure something did happen that involved ETs but what exactly occurred he couldn't recall.
>
> "We were taken to a place or possibly aboard a craft that had an environment put together specifically for the sake of resembling Earth...I feel that I am to tell you that this whole experience was *orchestrated!* We were put in situations for the sake of the results which were being accumulated in the room we were kept in. The technicians were out of view but I sensed them noting and documenting our every response. I felt both good and bad [during] this experience. It was as if the tests were divided into two groups. One gave good feelings and the other bad...
>
> Of particular interest was the thought [given to us] that we would not be returning to prison! All of us were extremely happy about this fact. In all of my ET experiences I have never entertained the notion that I would be going or taken with them until this night. I recall wondering what the prison authorities would do when they found me missing. I was overcome with joy about this thought. Sadly, I suspect we were told this just for the sake of the results — kind of cruel, huh?

If extraterrestrials are using our prisons as laboratories, the above experience would make a lot of sense. The ETs seem interested in emotions of a polarized nature — anger, fear, or joy. What better way to elicit a joyful response than by telling an inmate that he won't have to return to prison? This does not necessarily indicate that they are cruel, but perhaps just ignorant of the nature of our emotions. To them, our various emotions might just seem like different colored apples, and they are simply exploring the area of their curiosity.

In his communications to us, Leigh chose to reveal two more experiences told to him by his fellow inmates. As one could imagine, the inmates keep these experiences to themselves for fear that their psychological evaluations would be jeopardized. Leigh has built a trust with many such inmates, and so their stories are exchanged quietly between each other.

> One individual, who said that I could not use his name, had a pretty scary event happen to him about a year ago. It was late, somewhere near 2:30 a.m. He related that for some reason he awoke and because his bed is situated so that he can see out his window, upon opening his eyes he saw something "not of this world." (These are his words.) This being was staring into his room. Naturally, if you see something with a huge head and two great big black eyes staring at you through a window, you are going to let someone know. This is just what he did. He created such a furor that guards were ordered to search the living compound for an intruder. He related that the whole event was "just scary." Needless to say, nothing or no one was found. Positive, negative, or neutral? He called it a positively negative event that he hopes never happens again!
>
> Kevin said that he too saw something like an alien craft outside his window while in the sleep state. Actually he thought that he was awake when this occurred but after awakening in the morning he realized that he [had been] asleep. He also mentioned that one day, all day long, he had funny feelings in his right ear. Now, I have never told him that I too have these [sensations in my right ear] when I sense an unseen presence. Coincidence?

Perhaps not. Kevin's experiences recounted above regarding his right ear are not new to ufology. There have been a number of cases in which there has been bleeding from the nose or ear after an encounter. If these are in fact physical

105

encounters, how frequent are these occurring? Leigh, once again, speaks of his recollections.

> In my years of prison living, I have come across *many* individuals who have awakened in the morning to find blood on their pillows caused by a nosebleed sometime during the night. Way, way too many, according to my thinking. I have wondered about this for years!

So far, Leigh's accounts match up pretty nicely with the patterns displayed in a great deal of abduction research. the obvious question to be asked now is, "Who are these beings that the inmates are encountering?" The inmate who wishes to remain anonymous describes them as being large-headed with huge black eyes — your basic Zeta Reticuli in our method of labeling. Have there been any others? Here again the common pattern is displayed in Leigh's account.

> I was asleep but came awake while sleeping. I noticed that the sky was full of moving craft. These craft came into our area in two uniform formations. There were 18 to 20 of them. Half went about their business (whatever that was) while the other half continued to fly over the prison. While flying over, these craft were *all* emanating a green-blue beam. After watching for a time I realized that there was a reason for this light and their flight. They were searching for and identifying individuals. I was one. I felt myself being pulled by the light. I was now in a craft with others. Some I recognized from the prison; many I did not know.
>
> All that happened on board I do not recall, but a great deal I do. I was shown how a certain alien group was using the AIDS epidemic for their purposes and how they were manipulating the carriers to spread the disease. I was also show[n] how the mass media was being used to keep a form of control over huge numbers of people...My instructor was a female with red hair, and I remember telling myself that she wasn't half bad for an alien. To this she laughed and said, "I'll take that as a compliment."

> She knew my thoughts. She laughed a lot and was very
> free with the information given. She had deep dark liq-
> uid brown eyes and her teeth were small, coming to slight-
> ly rounded points.

Interesting. The first description of alien interaction involved the short, bald, large-eyed beings. The above encounter involved a humanoid being, perhaps the same species
as those encountered in similar cases. As in other cases, the
large-eyed being was more interested in taking samples and
running experiments. The encounter with the humanoid
seemed more for the purpose of giving information and
making direct contact. One statement that Leigh made to us
really hit home:

> I have the feeling that one group wants me to know what
> is going on...while the other does not.

What is going on? We posed some questions to the entity
Sasha regarding experiments conducted in controlled environments. What we received is far from complete, but may
be one step further in understanding the scope of the visitor
enigma.

* * *

*Please talk about abductions taking place in prisons. Would
you say it is occurring?*

Sasha: The experience that you call abduction is indeed
occurring in the prison system, but we would of course wish
to elaborate on this.

On one level, abductions within prisons exist neither more
nor less than within the general population. The abduction
situations are occurring for all of those who have agreed to
have that experience. On this level that we speak of, whether
they are in prison or not is irrelevant.

Some of the ET groups who are having interactions with inmates are not even aware that the inmates are part of a controlled society. Some ETs are aware of it, others are not. Also, it would depend upon which group you are speaking about.

There are several ET groups involved in the prison abductions. The first group (which would represent a minority of abduction experiences) would be what you consider the benign Zeta Reticuli.

The individual that you know of as Leigh is having encounters with the benign Zeta Reticuli group, among others.

Generally speaking, with any type of abduction experience, the nature of your consciousness is going to tell you the nature of your experience with the extraterrestrials. So if you are a fearful person, you are going to draw in fearful contact. If you are seeking spiritual growth, you will draw in a benign or benevolent contact experience.

The benign Zeta Reticuli group are aware these inmates are in a prison facility. They are communicating with these inmates for various reasons. One is to gather information about the human energetic field and the human emotional body in a confined environment — especially an environment with a lot of negativity. The Zeta Reticuli themselves are not generating the negativity; they are only studying the results of it.

Another reason for the abduction experience would be for the gathering of genetic material within a secluded environment. As odd as it may sound, the Zeta Reticuli are looking for mutations in genetics due to the seclusion that inmates encounter. In some ways they correlate the past underground seclusion of their race with the experience of these inmates. They wish to study the adaptation of inmates' genetics to their confined environment.

An additional reason for the interaction would be as a gift to some of these inmates — especially in interactions that are of a spiritual nature. In some ways the Zeta Reticuli feel a camaraderie of sorts; they remember the experience of seclusion in their past. This is another attempt at healing. So there is very much of an exchange with these more benign groups.

Another group having contact with inmates would be what we call the "data collectors." These would primarily be neutral Zeta Reticuli, but there may be some other species involved. These interactions are purely scientific in nature. They are neither negative or positive. They are not designed to give any spiritual enlightenment to the inmates. They are not designed to manipulate them, either. Contact is for the purpose of pure data collection. This is done within the general population as well, but it is done more frequently in the prison population because it is a controlled environment.

Other groups involved with inmate visitations are largely humanoid—comprised of various beings of Lyran descent (such as Pleiadian) and other types of humanoids from the same genetic strain. These are highly benevolent in nature. This would also represent a minority, and only individuals who are open to this type of contact will receive this contact. It is generally of a nature that has nothing to do with experimentation or tests, but with imparting knowledge to the inmates. Generally, the humanoid extraterrestrial giving the information will have a connection with the specific person being communicated with.

The final group we will discuss is of a negative nature. Let us explain. Within the abduction experiences of the general population, this negative group represents a very small percentage. In a controlled environment with a considerable amount of negativity such as a prison, the percentage of this group's interactions increases.

In the controlled environment of a prison, there are more interactions with this negative group than within the general population. The simple reason is that many are living in fear, powerlessness and victimization and will draw that type of communication or contact to them. These negative extraterrestrials would range from the negatively oriented Zeta Reticuli (which some call the Greys), to any type of Orion interaction—whether it be with physical extraterrestrials, telepathic contact, or holographic projections. There are also other mixed humanoids who are of a negative orientation. Generally, it is for the purpose of gathering data about the human psyche to use at a later date to perhaps exert control or power over the human species.

Also, because negatively oriented ETs recognize that these individuals are in a controlled environment, they are sometimes used as guinea pigs. Experiments that you might deem inhumane may be conducted. Because of the nature of the confinement, this percentage is higher in the prison population than it is within the general population.

All of these ET groups are aware of each other, and there is some inner politics between the groups. Some try to intervene and shield some of the inmates from the more negative groups. The negative groups may try to exert control over some inmates, thinking that if they keep them in fear they will no longer be able to contact a benevolent group. Again, these are small percentages, but we are speaking of the dynamics. It is important to remember here that all humans, despite their place in society, have chosen the reality they experience. Any negative ET encounters can be turned around by the power of the individual.

What about our own people doing experiments in the prisons?

That is another story we really do not wish to go into. It is being done. There are isolated pockets. It is not an overall occurrence from prison to prison.

Are there any methods or approaches used that are unique to the prison environment?

The methodologies or tools used in these contacts are not different per se, but some of the specifics are. Leigh talked about an experience he had where he was told he would not have to return to prison. That comment would not be something that would affect someone in the general population the way it affected him. Because the lives seem more limited within the prison population, they will study that feeling of limitation. The negatives, of course, will use that feeling of limitation to their benefit. The more positive ETs will seek to allow the inmates to feel less limited within their environment. That theme of limitation and confinement is engaged very much.

For what purpose?

The prison environment can be seen as a microcosmic representation of your entire planet. There have been many rumors about your Earth being the penal colony of the galaxy. This is not a reality in the sense that someone has done this to you. But this has been the emotional sensation or feeling that your planet as a whole has had. So the prison environment is a microcosm of the entire macrocosm of the mass consciousness. Therefore by working in the microcosm they can see the larger picture within the macrocosm.

Can you give some other examples with various groups about how they approach the environment? Who are they going to work with?

The benevolent group of humanoids target the individuals they communicate with by whom they can find. This means that they can "see" anyone who is vibrating at a certain level. A higher vibration means that the individual is coming out of the idea of victimization. Those individuals are the ones they can find. Those are the ones they seek, because they understand that those individuals represent a shift or a change in the entire prison population. That is why they are targeted.

The benign Zeta Reticuli and the data collectors both focus in on the person they can find. This time "who they can find" means which signature vibrations are programmed in their computer. So the next question would be, "How are the signature vibrations programmed into the computer?" The answer to that would simply be as stated in previous chapters about prior agreements, or be the idea of voluntary cooperation on the energy level.

The more negatively oriented groups will also target individuals they can find. Again it is the idea of like attracting like. The negatively oriented ETs can find those most closely like themselves — humans who are in fear, victimization, and who are preying on other people.

What about the more human ET groups? What about their motivation and their plans? What is their intent?

Let us say they are the crusaders of the future. They are seeking to help Earth liberate itself from itself. They see individuals in the prisons as being a prime target to help raise the vibration on Earth. If the vibrations can be raised within a prison, for instance, it will have a ripple effect in the mass consciousness. Targeting inmates may be the most difficult and challenging work, but many feel it is the most rewarding and has the greatest effect.

That's where the most leverage is.

Exactly. Some of these humanoids contacting inmates are also Earth's future Terran beings, going back in time and attempting to reform the prison system in contemporary time by a raise in consciousness.

Do you know of any humanoids yourself who do this? Can you give an example of a likely scenario?

Part of my training as a cultural engineer was in studying the penal system on your planet. This was not done through physical abduction of inmates. It was done through the voluntary cooperation of various souls who have chosen incarceration on Earth. These interactions took place mostly in their dream state. There were one or two situations where some of the researchers physically visited the cell of some of these inmates to engage in pure conversation. This is kept very quiet, obviously, because of certain evaluations that many of the inmates have to go through. I personally did not visit any of the cells, though some of my colleagues did.

And what transpired?

There was a communication between the two on a telepathic level that had to do with emotions, and the emotions that the inmate was feeling in their surroundings — a tapping into their desires, hopes and fears. There was a communication on the part of the extraterrestrial to the inmate of what you would consider to be perhaps cosmic information, perhaps spiritual information, metaphysical principles. This would allow the inmates to begin expanding their point of view. This is not something that I can talk about in more concrete ways, because it was a very abstract experience and interchange. Frequently in the astral or dream state some of the inmates are taken to other planetary environments or aboard ships to be given information. Sometimes the ETs even communicate with individuals they know on other levels. This is a joyful interaction, but at the same time it has significant benefits because when the inmate returns, they bring that energy of joy and cooperation with them.

What knowledge have the extraterrestrials gained from their interactions with the inmates, and what have the inmates gained? Not only in just the spiritual experience, but what do they remember?

The benevolent humanoid group benefits from these interactions because they are able to see their past, the times when they had penal systems, the times when they felt confined.

113

The emotions that are brought up and given to them by these generous inmates are very valuable for their growth.

The benign Zeta Reticuli on one level believe they are gathering data about the chemical evolution of the human body in times of emotional stress. They are learning more than that, however, because they are also healing their past through these interactions. That is something they have not really allowed themselves to understand at this point.

The data collectors are also gathering data regarding the chemical evolution of the human being in stressful circumstances. They are very interested in genetic evolution, so this information is of value to them because it will allow them to create, in their genetic work, stronger and stronger strains that are able to withstand a lot of stress and change.

The negatively oriented groups have a very interesting point of view on this. They believe that they are influencing the inmate population in a way that can be likened to infiltration. They believe they are infiltrating your society by starting with the inmate population. They feel it is an easy way in. But it's a dead end. They have not seen that. Negatively oriented groups seek expansion outside of themselves, which means domination over others.

Do these groups maintain observation programs with people they know are eventually going to prison?

Yes. We wouldn't say it is targeted at future prison inmates, but simply targeted at individuals who are motivated to commit crimes that may lead to incarceration. It's not incarceration itself that they are interested in; its just the emotional motivation the people are experiencing that is the target.

So they can find the same type of people outside of prison as on the inside?

Yes. However, once one is in prison then the whole situation changes, because it is a controlled environment.

I'd like to know how these groups view our penal system. Do they recognize the purpose of a prison right away? Maybe a more alien group would never even see its purpose.

Yes. The humanoid groups recognize the prison systems right away. In the Lyran races there have been whole planets that have been prisons. So the idea of punishment and prison is not something new.

Some of the other groups who are much further removed from this type of system are frequently not even aware of the concept of isolation. There are still some groups who are studying prisons and finding them to be an enigma compared to the rest of society. They have not grasped the concept. Some of these groups do not understand that prison is a forced separation. Recognize that you are dealing with some of these extraterrestrial groups who exist in a reality very different from yours. With that in mind, they do not understand the concepts that you have brought into physicality on your planet, such as forced isolation.

Is there ever a sense of judgment on the part of ETs?

It depends on which group you are talking about. In the lesser evolved groups, yes, there is a sense of judgment. In the more evolved groups, no. Some groups so totally removed from your reality cannot even understand the concept enough to judge it.

What do the inmates experience? What changes have occurred? If they read this transcript, what would they begin to make sense of?

Some of the obvious clues, especially with some of the more negatively oriented or unevolved groups, would be the recurring nosebleeds at night and the sense of emotional violation they can't explain. Some even experience missing time. There is also the sense of increased paranoia, even more than the prison environment would bring about. Those are some examples.

What about the more positive interactions?

Those would be indicative of an expanding awareness — a lessening of anger about the situation one is in. Perhaps a remembrance of dreams in which a lot of information or energy was exchanged. A sense of inner peace. A sense of movement/growth that was not there previously, and a sense of having a purpose.

What about other types of isolated environments, such as mental institutions?

We would say that within mental institutions you will find contact as well. The parameters with which contact is initiated or given would basically be the same as the prison environment. It would parallel the prison environment almost exactly because you are dealing with a type of isolationist energy, even if it is internal isolation (such as severe depression or catatonia).

Are the mental institutions seen as a unique opportunity to study some unusual aspects of humanity?

Yes. Some of the studies that have been done with mental institutions on the part of extraterrestrials are not that surprising, because very often what individuals in mental institutions experience is an overlap of reality — an interdimensionalality with which they do not know how to cope. As these individuals are being studied, there is an awareness that *they are mankind's pioneers who are learning to deal with interdimensional reality — a skill that all will soon need.*

So we could assume that Pleiadians and other humanoids would be more interested in behavior than the actual neurochemicals?

Yes. Exactly.

And the Zeta Reticuli would be more interested in neurochemicals?

Yes. It has been discussed that the Zeta Reticuli have deliberately altered themselves to stay in physical reality. Some of the data they have received has come from mental institutions. They have been able to see how one can exist multidimensionally and still be physical. This has allowed them to create ways in which they are able to stay physical.

Are there any helpful ideas that could be communicated to the prisoners who are dealing with negative scenarios?

Some of these have already been outlined in the book, but the thing to remember most is that people will attract what they are equal to. If someone is having negative extraterrestrial experiences while being incarcerated, we would say that the way to remove themself from that situation is to work on the integration of fear and victimization. As one does this, the negative extraterrestrial experiences cannot continue. So it comes right back down to the self. *A person can change the experience by whatever they can do to let go of the idea of victimization within the self.*

What about those prisoners who really aren't familiar with distinguishing between victimization and empowerment? Are there any symbolic ideas, such as colors, sounds, pictures, or symbols that can be of assistance?

Yes, we would say that placing blue light around the self in the auric field would be of benefit to someone who does not understand the concept of nonvictimization. This was given also in the chapter called "Changing the Abduction Experience." Eventually each abductee will need to come to terms with the idea of victimization.

We've presented information in this chapter that is literally the tip of the iceberg. There are many segments of your society affected or influenced by extraterrestrial contact.

These segments of society have been overlooked, so far, in the public's eye. Because there will be many revelations soon about the extraterrestrial experience, it is time now to understand that the extraterrestrial experience permeates every level of your society. You cannot lock yourselves away from it, for you will only draw it to you anywhere you go.

This information has been brought to you so you may see how many levels of contact are occurring in your society. Though there may be individual agendas within each group, the higher level purpose is for the evolution on your planet to occur. That is the bottom line. We present this information to encourage you to begin opening up the closets and looking in the hidden corners of your society where you have not yet looked. There is still much to discover.

8

The Metahuman Connection

"More than anything else that has occurred, the humanoid presence [during an abduction] has actually accelerated the evolution of the consciousness of abductees." — Germane

Many extraterrestrial contact stories relate the presence of humanoids working in cooperation with the Zeta Reticuli-type beings. Who are these humanoids? What is their interest in the abduction phenomenon?

We presented some of these questions to Germane. What follows are his responses as well as even more information about the future ramifications of the genetic experiments conducted on Earth during the last several thousand years.

* * *

Why have some abductees seen tall blonde humanoids on board spaceships during abduction experiences? Who are they? What is their genetic make-up? Where are they from? Just give us a basic foundation so we can set some parameters.

Germane: We are dealing with the limited aspects of your labeling in trying to give you a detailed picture. Sixty percent (average) of the blonde humanoid beings seen during these abduction experiences with the Zeta Reticuli come from the

119

future. The remaining 40% is not from the future but represents many other scenarios.

In terms of the genetic make-up of these humanoids from the future (the 60%), let us come up with labels that are applicable. We will give you three: meta-Lyran, meta-Pleiadian, and meta-Terran.

This comes under which percentage?

The 60% group.

What do you mean by "meta?"

"Meta," of course, means "beyond." Beyond Lyran, beyond Pleiadian, beyond Terran (Earth). This means that the genetic strains or origins of some of these beings were either Lyran, Pleiadian, or Terran. Their own evolutionary process has taken them beyond what you know of in contemporary contacts. Primarily you will find that these beings as a whole are able to manipulate energy and matter in a much more fluid way than the contemporary contacts you have now. It is another evolutionary step.

What do you mean by "manipulate energy and matter"?

They can manipulate their own form from energy to matter very easily. They can manipulate their own vibrational frequency.

So we are talking about their ability to make themselves dense in third density?

Yes. It is something that is very easy for them.

So they can alter their vibration but not necessarily their shape?

They do not necessarily alter their shape, but they can emit a vibratory frequency that will allow you as the perceiver to see them as something different from what they truly are.

Is this due to their fourth-density level? Or is it due to their personal talents and training?

A little bit of both. It is something that you will do in fourth density and cannot do in third. But it also has to do with these particular beings and what they've chosen in terms of their work. This has allowed them to focus on these abilities.

Do they have a cohesive identity? Do these meta-Lyrans, meta-Pleiadians, and meta-Terrans all group together?

They are grouped together. The labels we have given to you are very much for *you* and do not represent the way they see themselves. From their point of view (in your future), they are all one species.

From their point of view, are they all working toward the same goals?

Oh, yes. Their reality is very cohesive. Their beliefs are very cohesive. They have individual excitement, but they recognize how it all fits together.

The other 40% we spoke about represent either contemporary Pleiadian, contemporary Lyran, or hybrid races. When we say hybrid we are not talking about the hybrids the Zeta Reticuli are working on. We are referring more to crossbreeding—crosses between Lyran/Pleiadian and other subraces. Some are crosses between Pleiadian and Earth human. We cannot really give you categories that exist within that 40% because it really is a melting pot.

The difference is that those coming from the future are more integrated genetically than those coming from the more contemporary contacts.

What, if any, are the differences in the intent of the two groups and how they view their own purpose?

We will label the meta-Lyran, meta-Pleiadian and meta-Terrans as simply "metahuman" all right? The metahuman intent is the stimulation of evolution. You might call them evolutionary engineers.

The intent of the 40% contemporary group is different for each group. Mostly, it has to do with contact. It may have to do with genetic research or the fulfillment of agreements of a future self to a past self (such as a Pleiadian visiting his or her past self on Earth). The purposes are different for each individual.

Why do these interactions occur?

The metahuman group from the future has several different agendas, but they are all intertwined. This has to do with stimulating the energy necessary in the individual or the mass-conscious mind of a society to trigger the evolutionary process — to make the leap. They have been known as the ones who, coming from the future, instigated the creation of the Asian races on your planet. They will also be present and active as the Zeta Reticuli resolve their genetic problems. They will be present and active as the Zeta Reticuli abandon their dying line and move into the new race they are creating through the hybrid experiments.

On a more personal level in terms of the abduction experience, these humanoids also serve several functions. The metahumans serve as a conduit between the human detainee and the Zeta Reticuli consciousness the human is interacting with. They may act as an empath. The Zeta Reticuli, even in this future, have not yet mastered the understanding of emotions, but they have learned the value of using empaths to translate to them what the human is experiencing. The humanoids take the emotional expressions from the human, synthesize them into a form that the Zeta Reticuli can identify with, and channel those emotions through themselves so that the Zetas can understand.

Are we talking about the full spectrum of thoughts or only certain parts of emotionality?

Certain parts of emotionality.

There are many cases where there is very good communication between the Zetas and an abductee.

Exactly. This is a more subtle form of communication. It may also be a type of communication that you would call conversation rather than just emotional communication.

Case studies have stated that the abductees have felt at home with the more humanoid extraterrestrials. Is that because of the human quality?

Not only because of the human quality; you will find in nature that animals on your world instinctively know when other creatures have genetic links to them. There is a recognition on the part of the Earth human that there is a very direct and solid genetic connection to these metahuman beings. They do not feel this same type of connection to the Zeta Reticuli. That is where the familiarity comes in. The physical appearance also adds to the comfort of the detainee.

Is a humanoid from either the 60% or the 40% group present during every abduction by the Zeta Reticuli?

They are not present in every abduction.

So there are abduction experiences where just the Zetas are involved?

Yes.

What would determine whether one of these humanoids would be present?

It would really depend on the project that is being done. Generally speaking, the Zeta Reticuli are the instigators of the project and they would be the ones who decide what beings are present for what interaction. The lesser evolved Zeta Reticuli beings will, 99% of the time, not desire the metahuman to be present. The more evolved in consciousness the Zetas become, the more likely they are to request the presence of these beings.

So it is currently happening in a very low ratio.

It is a low ratio, but it is growing. Again, it will depend on the orientation of the Zeta Reticuli you are dealing with. Right now you are having the conflict between the negatively oriented ones on one side and the benevolent, love-and-light ones on the other — as well as everything in between. The experience is really quite unique for each Zeta group conducting experiments.

How did this start? Who initiated it?

First of all, you will not get Zetas to admit that they have emotions. But you could say that groups of Zetas have become increasingly frustrated because of the chasm they felt between themselves and the humans with whom they were interacting. So they realized that they needed a conduit. They then contacted some of the more rebel Lyran/Pleiadian subgroups to assist. This became a very profound research project for both the metahumans and the Zeta Reticuli, which allowed their personal evolution to occur very rapidly. It was actually the understanding or recognition — you may call it frustration — that they were not achieving anything that led them to seek assistance in other directions.

Give me a scenario that may have happened to illustrate how this was set up. For instance, how did the crew of one ship (or the authority network of the Zeta Reticuli) contact someone else to help them?

First of all, there is the Association of Worlds, which is the basic agreed-upon group that represents the mother organization. There are satellite organizations affiliated with the Association, and then there are more revolutionary groups that have their own version of the Association.

These groups are not in conflict with each other. They may not embrace what each other stands for, but they are not in conflict. The Zeta groups encounter in their circles some of the satellite and revolutionary groups, and they know specific individuals within those groups from whom they solicit assistance.

How would they ask for this assistance? How was the inquiry made?

The inquiry is made telepathically. The concepts are sent as a telepathic impulse or "thought ball" that is received by all individuals the impulse is aimed at. Those who are excited about the idea answer the call.

What concepts were used when communication was established? What did the Zetas "say"?

Again, it is not so much what they said; the concept communicated was, "Our race is dying out. Your race will too unless we do something about it." It was not so much that the Zetas were playing on the humanoid fear of extinction, but it was very logically packaged, shall we say.

The rebel groups understood the value of working with them not only to broaden the gene pool, but also to gain more knowledge. Most individuals do not turn down that kind of offer.

Let us say, for instance, that there is a group of Pleiadians observing Zeta Reticuli activities here, and they try to communicate with the Zetas to get them to stop or alter their approach. They offer to go on board to assist the Zeta Reticuli in getting what they need in a more efficient way. At the same time, they make it smoother and more fruitful.

That is one idea that is accurate. That example is more indicative of the future metahumans than the 40% group.

What do the Zeta Reticuli think they can gain from having humanoids present during their interactions with us?

They can gain many different things. One is that they can observe the humans and the metahumans and compare their behavior. They have learned a lot of information this way. We cannot stress that enough. Those interactions have given them breakthroughs in understanding frequency and the emotional body. In seeing the difference between the human and the metahuman, they actually can touch their past in a much more real way than they were ever able to before. That was the primary thing of value for them.

Another reason has to do with the future of the genetic project that has not happened yet on Earth. Eventually the humans that were taken began to fight back — to awaken and snap out of the paralysis. Once they awakened, it was a highly traumatic experience (even more than it would have been otherwise). This was disturbing to the Zetas. Their understanding was that if there were humanoids present, it wouldn't be as traumatic. Again they were correct. More than anything else that has occurred, however, the humanoid presence [during abductions] has actually accelerated the evolution of the consciousness of abductees.

What do the humanoids gain from this arrangement?

Again you must understand that we must speak in generalities because each group has its own desires. They are always looking for ways to rectify their past. So the humanoids see this as a way to give back to humans what they perceive they've removed from Earth for thousands of years.

We are not justifying this. We are simply telling you that this is what they feel. Do you understand what we mean by that? It is a way to be of service that they perceive is not direct interference. Since the Zetas are interfering already, they are softening it. They are turning the interference into evolution — that is the way they see it.

126

Is this type of abduction going on all over the galaxy?

No, it is not.

So it is unique that some other group is able to abduct us during the night. These humanoids must see somehow that this is so because of our distorted past — our abused species childhood. Therefore they want to interact with that, to give us something we were lacking in a way that does not interfere?

Yes.

And this is how they can engage our dysfunction without taking our power away or enabling us to continue our dysfunction.

Yes. There will also be personal reasons for each individual who is involved, but as a whole, it is the humanoids' understanding that they are giving you a gift in return.

Give me some examples of what actually goes on when a human is taken on board a Zeta Reticuli craft and a humanoid is present there. Is there only one humanoid? Are they male or female?

Sometimes there are more than one, and they can be male or female. Who is present is determined by the belief system of the human taken on board. The belief systems can be discovered by a very brief energy scan. Some are more secure with females and some are more secure with males.

How do the metahumans get to the specific time and location of the Zeta interaction with the human? Is teleportation involved?

They are all contained on the Zeta ship. For example, there is a Zeta ship with a Zeta crew. There is also a metahuman crew on board. The individual beings interacting with a certain abductee will be chosen from that crew as the abductee comes aboard.

127

I see. So there is a metahuman pool of talent constantly on the ship from which one or two will interact during any particular abduction experience. Could they be on board their own mission ship nearby?

That is a possibility also. They are nearby in time and space. There is a pool of individuals who are the primary staff members, let us say. They are chosen from that pool.

Go on with what happens when a person is brought on board.

Here is a scenario to answer your question. It will be simplified because the experience is much more abstract.

There is a human brought in, who is seated in a chair or put on a table. The Zeta beings are the primary scientists conducting experiments. During this time the chosen metahuman crew links themselves empathically with the human subconscious and follows the flow of their emotions and their mental pictures.

Frequently these metahumans attempt to maintain a sense of stability with the emotional energy. But at times they are not able to hold the link and the human awakens. At this point the duty of the metahumans is to make their presence known, which of course has a calming affect. Sometimes they place their hands on the human – on the head or on the hand. They may speak soothingly to the human telepathically or physically. Whatever the case, the purpose is to allow the detainee to feel comfortable and relaxed.

During these types of interactions the Zetas observe the communication between the metahuman and the human and gain data that is added to their bank of information. That is an example.

Would this same basic scenario occur with the other 40% group – not the metahumans, but the contemporary humanoids?

There are more variations in this 40% group. You may find that some of the humanoid groups actually give you a tour of the ship, speak to you of their home world, be much more present as a real person. You may also find that — depending on the scenario — they may actually ask the human questions. This isn't so much to gain data from you, but to learn about how you perceive reality.

For instance, in the Betty and Barney Hill case on your world, one of the questions asked by the Zetas was, "What is yellow?" Betty attempted to describe what yellow was. That was a question about perception. One of the things they may do is ask several people what yellow is, and watch the variation in response.

Communication with this 40% group is much more direct and face-to-face. The interaction in the 60% group — the metahumans — can be more symbolic, more archetypal, more energetic.

Do the 40% (humanoid) and the 60% (metahuman) groups ever mix?

That really depends on the situation. Generally, no. But there may be individuals from the 40% group who desire a more accelerated or evolved interaction. They may then choose to work with the group from the future. It depends on the orientation of the metahuman. The labeling is very difficult for us to work around.

What type of communication goes on between the mediating humanoids and the Zeta Reticuli?

The communication is telepathic — not telempathic in terms of emotional communication. It is mental communication.

That is where their training would have to come in.

Exactly. These metahumans must have abilities in both telempathy and telepathy.

129

Humans are naturally telempathic, but not so skilled at telepathy?

Yes. These metahumans have this as part of their training. The communication that occurs will be different for each situation. One example is that the metahuman may actually be relaying mentally to the Zeta the vital signs of the human detainee. They may also relay information such as, "At this moment the human is experiencing an internal fear scenario about nuclear war." This way the Zetas can measure the internal emotional experience of the human with the body reactions at the same time.

Are they clarifying the divisions of identity in the detainee (for instance, the subconscious, unconscious and conscious mind)? The Zeta Reticuli are not very adept at recognizing these levels of being.

Yes, correct. For instance the metahuman may say, "The human is experiencing a level of fear from the subconscious that the human is not aware of in the conscious state." That way the Zeta can begin understanding the divisions humans have between levels of their consciousness.

Let us talk about the detainee. Is there any advice you could give in case they encounter a metahuman during an abduction?

If this occurs, we would certainly suggest that one make the best of it. Squeeze every little bit of information and communication out of it that you can if you are capable of doing so.

Are there any cases of negatively oriented humanoid beings involved with the Zeta abductions?

Within the 40% group, there is a very small percentage of negatively oriented humanoids. This would happen only if the Zetas themselves are of a negative orientation. It is very rare. It is our understanding that the humanoid present

130

would not be of the metahuman type but of a lesser evolved species that although humanoid, does not have the focus of their own evolution as the top priority. It is very, very rare.

We are being told that it has occurred with some negatively oriented Orion beings paired with some of the renegade Zeta Reticuli who took refuge in the Orion system. These negatively oriented humanoids were genetically not Lyran, but Vegan-based, from which the Orions come. There are encounters such as this that are recorded, we are told. They are not "fun," in your words.

Do the other humanoids (Lyrans and Pleiadians) react in a protective way when this occurs? Do they come to the rescue of the human?

It has been known to happen, but sometimes it does not because of the codes of noninterference.

They have grappled with the whole interference concept, as you know. If you watch someone being kidnapped and you assume the person being kidnapped is a victim, you must then assume that they have not chosen their reality. If you have that belief, then you may feel it is your responsibility to save them. But when you begin to understand that all beings *do* choose their reality (whether or not they are aware of it), then the question comes back to you, "Do I interfere? Is my interference part of the co-created choice that the kidnappee and myself have made?" Depending on the different metahuman orientations, the negatives may thus be confronted.

And sometimes they perceive it is part of the agreement to...

Interfere. And sometimes not. It is really dependent upon the individual circumstances.

Do you have anything to say about the background of the Oriental races?

131

We will tell you a little story that will help you to understand how long the genetic project has been worked on during your Earth's development, where it is going, and the significance of its beginning. We have spoken in the past about the beginnings of your planet. We've also talked about how your forefathers attempted to attain a balanced, peaceful society. Because of the diversity within the society, that peace was never attained.

When the seeding of Earth began, the intention was that Earth would be the place of integration — the planet of peace. The original races who were the ones allowed to flourish on Earth were all who are present now *except* the Oriental races. We stop here in the story and we jump ahead millennia.

The Association of Worlds and the original forefathers of your planet (some of whom are now evolved beyond physicality) looked back at the probability line that was created through their genetic work. They saw that the unification and integration they desired did not work. They needed to go back to the beginning and insert something that would change the probability they saw you moving toward. In this future there were groups controlling the genetic project on Earth. These groups (a joint effort between the future Zeta Reticuli and the metahuman beings) then went back in time on your Earth. They inserted the genetics into your evolutionary line that would allow for the creation of the Asian races on Earth.

If you look at the characteristics of the Asian races, you will find that there is a smaller amount of diversity. The concentration on individuality is not there. There is also a sense (as you see in your Eastern religions) of a deep and solid inner spirituality. These were the key elements needed to bring about the probable reality on Earth that was desired.

So now the time track that you are on is different from the one it once was. Now your diversity will not destroy you. Now there is a factor introduced into your planet's evolution which, down the line, will allow you all to integrate your beliefs and genetics into a solid and stable single race consciousness on Earth.

The Asian races have had some pretty extreme negative qualities.

There are extreme negative qualities in *all* races on Earth. There are positive qualities as well.

Where does their tendency to depopulate themselves as a matter of political practice come from?

This comes from the idea of seeing themselves as a single entity. Therefore a person does not represent an individual. This reflects the more dominant group aspect. It is seen as only a part of the whole and can be sacrificed for the good of the whole.

For instance, if your leg gets wounded and you cannot use it anymore, you can either drag it around or you can remove it if you perceive it is a hindrance. We are certainly not justifying what has occurred; we are simply attempting to explain to you the rationale that the archetypal Asian mind set would have about unity rather than individuality.

These positive and negative qualities of all the races will eventually come to balance. Right now they must be expressed for the energy to be triggered so that they may come to balance.

When you talk about creating one race on Earth, are you talking about the physical appearance becoming the same?

Not necessarily.

Are we going to lose the skin-color differentiation, for example?

We are speaking more about a mind set. There are always recessive genes that are going to come out. Because of who you are, you are always going to have variation in skin tone,

133

in hair and eye color. We are speaking more about the racial mind set of becoming one race.

Along similar lines, what is the difference between a meta-Terran and an Essassani?

Not much. Meta-Terran would be identified with Terra — Earth. They will not have the same type of genetic manipulation or experimentation that the Essassani had during their creation.

The Essassani are not part of the 60% group? Are they involved as humanoids in these abductions?

Some are, if the idea excites them, but we would not say it is a popular Essassani project.

Where the similarity lies is the racial mind set. The Essassani see themselves as one people. The meta-Terrans see themselves as one people. There is a similarity in the racial mind set.

I would think that the meta-Terran and the Essassani don't see themselves as one people together. Correct?

To make a differentiation such as that you would have to look into the past. The Essassani do not do that.

That would be the quality that would define us as Earth humans. That is the distinguishing mark of this branch of humans — our perception of history. I get the feeling that the meta-Terrans you are speaking about are very far into the future.

Yes, between 2,000 and 10,000 years.

I didn't think there were going to be humans around that long.

Some will chose to keep "receptacles" for consciousness. It is a different type of life and existence.

I have some unformed theories that species have clocks like a physical body does that would dictate how long they survive.

The metahuman is very far removed from Homo sapiens. The clock will have run out on Homo sapiens.

A natural metamorphosis? Or were there additional DNA codes inserted from ET groups?

When additional DNA codes are inserted from other groups, that can be considered a natural metamorphosis because it is natural for this to occur. The genetic manipulation of species is natural in the sense that it is has always been done. An unaltered metamorphosis can occur, but it would take longer. These metahumans can be considered a species that will exist very far into the future.

It will be very difficult to identify with that species, true?

Yes, except on a two-dimensional level. You can't yet see all the facets of it. Your reality does not possess the concepts.

Would an abductee feel the same genetic association with a meta-Terran as with an Essassani?

They would, in general, feel the connection more strongly with the meta-Terran. Again, it would be the genetic recognition.

There are many who protest what is occurring with abductions and genetic experiments. Those who protest can only protest when they feel they are victims. Those who feel they are not victims will not protest. Do you follow what we mean? The act of protestation means that in some way there must be a feeling of victimization.

It is time on your planet now to recognize that *nothing* happens to you from another source. *You are the source generating all experiences that you have.* You are at a bridge now. This bridge is leading you to the future evolution on Earth. If the Zeta Reticuli and all the other extraterrestrials were to

135

leave your planet now, this future would still occur. You are destined to evolve. *You are destined to become the species that has long been awaited.*

Your resistance and your fear will only prolong your evolution. Evolve you will. In the ancient days on your Earth, man who was dying out and making way for the more advanced version felt the same primal emotion that you feel now — the fear of annihilation. This is a fear of changing what you are, and being unable to recognize yourselves. It is a natural fear. The only way for you to make peace with this fear is to *trust the natural process of evolution.*

Each day allow yourselves to trust your own personal evolution a little bit more. Within your lifetimes you will have definitive proof of the leap that you are all taking toward the future evolution that you seek.

9

First Contact

"Because their reality is so alien to yours, the only way at this point that you can synthesize their energy is by starting at the archetypal level."   — Sasha

Long ago in the memory of ancient man, our dreams and visions were real. We conducted our lives, raised our children, and hunted our food. On top of these necessities of life, we also had a rich spirituality based on the inner world of symbols. When a young apprentice had a shamanistic vision, he *knew* the experience was symbolic and not literal. He also knew how to interpret that archetypal symbolism into a meaning for his own life. By allowing these experiences validity, he acknowledged the other levels of consciousness and sought to bring them into balance with his waking self.

Somewhere along the way we have begun to invalidate our inner world. The path of the shaman — according to the present Western world's point of view — is the path of pagans. The Western world looks to these poor pagans as perhaps Third Worlders, hoping maybe one day they will become "civilized." But what if we Westerners are the ones who have lost our true humanity? What if this inner world of symbols is vital to the human experience? The question would then become,

"What happens when we repress the inner world of vision and symbolism?"

Perhaps this inner world must then find other ways of expressing itself — leaking out into our daily lives in disguised ways. The more "civilized" we have become, the more unexplained phenomena we have experienced in our realities. It is quite possible that we've attracted the visitor phenomenon (as well as other unexplained events) as a way to bleed off the repressed energy from our inner world of the unconscious.

What follows is a dialog with Sasha, who gives information about contact programs that occurred in other star systems. She presents two case studies of opposite polarities — a society who was open to ET contact, and one who resisted it. Later she addresses the effect human contact is having within the Zeta Reticuli psyche.

* * *

Sasha: The methods by which your civilization has created contact with races such as the Zeta Reticuli are quite unique and are a product of your own development here on Earth. Your contact with the Zeta species is an indication, at this point in your development, that you are about to make a species leap.

When such leaps occur, you draw situations to you that have been outside of your normal parameters of reality. Your civilization has existed for several thousands of years with a fluctuating point of view about extraterrestrial contact. Throughout history, people did not believe extraterrestrials were a conceptual reality at all but instead seen as evidence of demons. During your current period of time, this contact indicates an actual acceleration of your evolutionary rate — transcendence, if you will — from one form of life to another.

The methodologies by which you have created this type of Zeta contact are diverse compared to other civilizations. For instance, you have manifested physical sightings in your skies.

You have manifested abduction experiences. You have manifested face-to-face contact as well as dream-state contact. You have manifested what could be considered traditional psychic phenomena regarding ET contact. You have thus manifested a representation of contact in both the physical and nonphysical realms.

Let us use the example of a garden hose. The water flows freely through this hose. The water represents the natural process of evolution. Let us say that the garden hose becomes blocked and the pressure builds up. There needs to be a way for this blockage to be released. Either the pressure can become so great that it will remove the blockage itself, or weaknesses in the hose will break portions of the hose apart so the water can burst forth and release the pressure.

The experiences on your world now that are acclimating you to the idea of ET contact are like these little holes in the hose through which the water is being pushed. It is a release of pressure from something that your civilization has denied for quite some time.

The way you have manifested contact seeping into your conscious minds is unique to your planet because of who you are. Other planets manifest their first contact with different methodologies. Yours is perfect for who you are. Ultimately, we would not judge that you are doing it in a wrong or right way. Simply, it is *your* way.

Using the analogy of the hose, is there something unnatural about the way we are manifesting contact?

What is unnatural is actually the forming of the blockage itself. For instance, the natural flow of the water symbolizes a natural spiritual evolution that allows you to gradually expand your consciousness from individual to societal to global to interplanetary perspectives. If there are any fears or ideas that you are not facing, they form the blockages in the hose. The "weaknesses" breaking through are simply the areas you are *not* protecting.

The other ways that the contact is manifested (through windows and back doors in the consciousness) seem to be natural aspects of who we are. The whole spectrum seems to be natural. And yet it is also a spectrum that we've denied.

Yes. It is manifesting itself according to who you are.

So in a sense it is manifesting according to our denial, not our acceptance.

Yes, it can be looked at that way. If you were of an accepting nature, there would be no need to create blockages nor to break through various portions of the hose. Other civilizations are different in the ways they manifest first contact. Let us explore two case studies with you.

These case studies are taken from first-contact mission-team accounts from our race and others within the Association. The purpose of this is to demonstrate to you the differences in how societies evolve themselves toward embracing ET contact.

ALPHA-3

We will label the first example as Alpha-3. This planetary species was initially begun by the seeding of Lyran-based groups and left alone to develop its natural species identity. It was not necessary for this species to know throughout its evolution that they were seeded by a source external to their planet. It was not necessary because there was no longer any interaction with the seeding race. The Alpha-3 society was allowed a very free and natural evolutionary process untainted by any of the galactic dramas.

They naturally progressed through time to a stage of developing technology. During this time they developed equal balance between technology and spirituality, so they were expanding at a balanced rate. One could say that Alpha-3 was a textbook case of planetary evolution. In that sense it had very little drama and was well orchestrated.

There was a period when this civilization became able to achieve space travel. Prior to this time they were watched very closely by some members of neighboring planetary systems. Before they actually left their planet, they were openly contacted. Let us describe this further.

Stage One

There are generally three stages of contact that occur with a species such as this. The first stage is telepathic contact with inhabitants of the planet. This is carried out approximately 50-100 years before the next stage is introduced. Telepathic contact is made with receptive individuals within the society. The telepathic contact is *not* saying, "We are here." It is instead a filtering of ideas about extraterrestrial beings that seemingly enter the imagination of the recipient and the normal flow of their life. This is reflected in society as, for instance, fictional works such as books that introduce the society to this idea.

Would this also include archetypal contact through symbology?

Yes. It is on the unseen levels of the humanoid mind.

Stage Two

Stage two is contact of a physical nature with the inhabitants when the physical crafts of other civilizations are seen in the skies. This is not presented in a threatening way. It is usually presented where there are large gatherings of people so that it becomes very quickly known.

Often there will also be experiences with these physical crafts. For example, let us say there is a forest fire that is very difficult to contain. The ET crafts come by and assist the firefighters to put out the fire; then they disappear. This is a demonstration of benevolence and is continued for a span of perhaps 25 years. Then stage three is initiated.

141

Stage Three

Stage three takes advantage of the progress made in stage two. After one of these instances when the craft had actually assisted with a disaster, the craft would land and come face to face with some of the inhabitants of the planet. That is first contact.

Those are the three main stages. The species from Alpha-3 encountered contact in such a fashion with no resistance or fear. It was simply a natural expression of evolution on a planetary scale.

We've had all three stages simultaneously going on throughout our history, yes?

Yes, but stage two was not implemented on your planet in the same way because of your psychological make-up.

Stage one is still one of the most important phases going on. Did these people have dreams? What did they experience in their internal world?

Their dreams did not display alien creatures. Instead, their dreams had emotional content that went beyond what they were used to. They were filled with symbology. For instance, a dream may have an individual flying through the stars. Perhaps they come face to face with someone while they are flying. (These are very simple examples.) The person they contact in the dream will look like their own species. There is no sense of alienness. The alienness that you feel on your world is a reflection of the alienness you feel between each other. The inhabitants of Alpha-3 did not start out feeling there is anything "alien" going on.

So they were not a people who experienced alienation amongst themselves?

Correct.

Did they experience astral travel to other planets or realms?

Yes, but it was all within the context of their own reality structure, so it never seemed alien.

Did they experience astral travel from ETs into their dream worlds?

Technically yes, but they had no way of knowing they were aliens.

During stage one, did the manifestation of astral contact take on a different theme?

Yes. The flavor of the astral contact in stage one began to demonstrate clearly and directly the idea of life and consciousness external to their world structure — not *alien*, but external.

So the boundaries of their world simply expanded?

Exactly.

Did their stage-one experiences synchronize smoothly with the visual sightings of craft in stage two?

Yes. Within stage one the species first began with more abstract ideas of contact, which then filtered down into the physical reality. For instance, in your society it would be translated as having books and movies that dealt in a positive, expanding way with the subject matter. During 50 to 100 years of this, the species then adopted a belief system that this was natural. Therefore, the first actual physical sightings in stage two were not a source of shock but a natural progression. They were also a source of great excitement.

So when they saw them, it was more a reaction of familiarity.

Exactly.

Did Alpha-3 have members of their own society who functioned as sociologists or philosophers who interpreted this phenomenon?

143

They had members of their society — sociophilosophers, if you wish to call them that — who talked about the expanding boundaries of their society, but did not talk about these ships as meaning something symbolically. That would have meant the ships were outside of their reality. The ships were not *alien*. It was not like looking at something that seemingly doesn't belong and trying to figure it out, like your society does. The process was so natural and gradual that there was no reason to philosophize about it.

So the reason we try to interpret it is because we deny it.

Exactly. You see it as something unnatural. You see it as an aspect of your reality that is alien. It is the same reason why you attempt to interpret your dreams. You see your dreams as being alien to who you are.

So maybe an integral idea of helping us to explore this is to examine the idea of interpretation. We seem to be interpreting everything we come across. Are you saying that these people did not interpret their experience?

Correct. They did not question it, because it did not exist *outside* of them.

In stage two, when they saw these ships in the sky, did they know there were people inside who were from another planet?

Yes. Absolutely no question. It was accepted.

Were they curious about it? Did they want to meet them?

They were curious and excited. There were times of celebration when these ships would appear — not because they saw these ships as superior to them, but simply because they had been conditioned to accept the positivity of this experience. It was simply a source of great excitement. There was no resistance whatsoever. There was no fear, and no arguments between individuals in their society.

144

Was there verbal contact in stage three before physical contact occurred?

No.

So stage two, which was purely visual, went right into stage three by the very act of a ship landing around the people and the occupants walking out and physically meeting the people on the planet?

Yes. Remember that stages one, two and three are superimposed over each other. During stage two, stage one is still occurring. They are not replaced by each other. So when stage two begins, the imaginative processes, the fiction, is still occurring. In this process they've already imagined the contents of the ships and the nature of the entities. Thus when the ships land in stage three, there is no surprise or fear. There is only acceptance and excitement.

It is kind of like being a Native American civilization and knowing that just over the ridge there is another community because you can see their smoke signals. You know they are there. Sometimes you send smoke signals back and forth to each other. But the day you meet is a celebration. Anything further on Alpha-3?

It seems pretty cut and dried. It is nothing like what occurs here!

Some of these stages occur here, but because of the level of resistance that your planet has, these stages have had to be altered. The resistance your planet is experiencing comes from your thousands of years of intermittent extraterrestrial contact as a primitive species.

BETA-4

Now then, we will share with you information about a culture that we will call Beta-4. Beta-4 is a civilization whose genetic connections are Vegan in nature. Their resistance to

145

ET contact was very, very strong. They have a lot of fear. Let us give you their background.

Beta-4 began as a penal colony. There were no prison structures built; instead they were simply abandoned there. They were not left with a lot of equipment or knowledge. After a period of time they degenerated somewhat. Their population grew very rapidly and segmented itself. They later came together and began forming a planetary identity.

When they came together, they retained no knowledge of their origins except through mythology. However, there was an underlying emotional memory that was a reaction to the abandonment they had experienced as the early penal colony. This created in them an unconscious desire to have nothing to do with those who abandoned them.

After thousands of years of evolution, they developed a society that utilized technology. When they were approaching planetary consciousness, they then began to question the idea of whether to build devices to take themselves off the planet. The species pain was still there concerning their abandonment, so the drive to go back out into space was not strong. They had an intense curiosity to see what was out there, but at the same time the pain they felt thinking about it kept them from building any machines to take them off the planet.

Using the garden-hose analogy, because they were unwilling to look at this pain, they formed a blockage. This blockage stopped the natural flow of species evolution. The inhabitants of Beta-4 were ready at this point to be indoctrinated into the galactic community. The extraterrestrials who began coming to their planet knew it would be challenging to assimilate that planet to the greater reality. They knew there would be resistance.

The extraterrestrials began simply by flying ships into areas where there were many people. The ships were never seen. Their focus in perception was so tight that the Betans literally *could not* perceive the reality of these ships.

146

This was a period when there was still a lot of conflict going on between the Lyran and Vegan empires. The extraterrestrials who were attempting communication with Beta-4 were aware that there was a possible threat coming because of these conflicts. It was imperative that contact be made. However, they tried many different ways to make contact but were unsuccessful. They tried landing; they tried approaching people. What ensued between the extraterrestrials and the Betans could be compared to a comedy on your world. It was as if they could not speak the same language. Any conversations made between these ETs and the Betans created total, absolute confusion.

From the point of view of the Betans, they were being talked to by a member of their own race. This member somehow was not able to communicate clearly. The Betan would simply walk away in confusion. The Betans would not see these ETs as being anything other than members of their own race. It was total limited vision. These encounters would shake the Betans very deeply internally, but because it was so abstract they would not discuss it amongst themselves. This phenomenon became something that could not enter the parameters of their reality.

Upon further consideration by the visiting extraterrestrials, it was understood that external attempts were fruitless. The next stage was to make internal attempts at communication. Originally the ETs had skipped the internal stages because the they thought the external stages would be more effective. However, they realized that they needed to utilize more internal methods of communication. This is where it becomes very surreal.

They began by entering the dream state of the Betans. Night after night every Betan was bombarded with dream imagery and communication from this ET intelligence. The Betans deliberately resisted this information, and a strain on their psyches was created. It got to the point where the pressure was so great that — using the garden-hose analogy — there had to be a bursting point.

The bursting point manifested itself as what you call "poltergeist activity." Strange things began happening in the reality of just about every individual on the planet. First it began with the individuals who were more spiritual in nature because they were the more receptive. Then it happened to every member of society. Translating this into your reality, this poltergeist phenomenon would take the form of strange images on the television, confusing messages printed on computer screens, and bizarre recordings on magnetic tape. These manifestations were created by the Betans' own minds as they attempted to hold back the communication. The phenomenon was not created by the extraterrestrials themselves. The psychic energy the Betans were withholding was actually being channeled into other media through which the communication could occur.

It got to the point where the stress became too much. When this occurred, the entire framework of their reality paradigm crumbled. It would be as if they were walking outside and everything was normal, and suddenly they felt a disorientation and then experienced a blackout or fainting spell; when they woke up, their reality paradigm was different. Suddenly they were able to see the ships. They were able to communicate between each other about what was going on. The ships remained in the distance for some time until individuals on Beta-4 were able to talk amongst themselves about the reality of this extraterrestrial presence. Then the ETs began to come closer.

Did the Betans think they were going mad?

Yes. Each individual, not wanting to talk about it, felt an extreme amount of stress which got worse and worse.

Now you have two examples of contact scenarios within your galactic family. One may ask then, "How do we on Earth fit into this?" Again, you are not as clear-cut. The examples we gave were of two civilizations who were of opposite polarity. Using the Alpha-3 contact program as an example, you are receiving stage one and stage three. Stage two has deliberately been altered for you because of your past dependence on extraterrestrial assistance.

Comparing you to the Beta-4 contacts, you experience a great amount of fear on archetypal levels that results in your shutting down to the reality of many things. Those of you experiencing the most fear on your planet are literally not seeing these physical ships when they are present.

The Zeta Reticuli are using stage one of the Alpha-3 program and to some degree, stage three. They are not so much interested in stage two. The Pleiadian civilizations in the past have been the ones to interact with you in the stage-two scenario.

The Zeta Reticuli are not really interested in stage one. They want to go right to stage three, but they must go through stage one.

Yes. Because their reality is so alien to yours, the only way at this point that you can synthesize their energy is by starting at stage one on the archetypal level.

As we experience the visitor phenomenon, sometimes it must come to us and we must interact with it within the parameters of our archetypal realities, our elemental realities, and within the deep parts of our minds that we've pushed down and denied. We must go to that stage to meet them. We experience many things that we don't know how to incorporate into our daily lives. Do the visitors also experience to some degree what we are experiencing? Is communicating with us a new experience for them? Do they come into our reality thinking they are going to take some samples and then all of a sudden they experience archetypes, elementals, and denied realities?

You are affecting the Zeta Reticuli in the same way they are affecting you. You have heard it stated that both of you

149

are facing your innermost primal fears as you deal with each other. This is the case. The way it manifests for the Zeta Reticuli is that at times their group mind will have the sensation or the illusion of experiencing individuality. It is kind of like a fantasy or a species dream about individuality. It is extremely shocking to their mass mind.

Would it be like a hallucination?

It is like a spontaneous thought that is quite intense.

So it is not simply the contactees experiencing archetypal fears. The visitors also experience their archetypal aspects when they contact us.

Yes. And we would say at this point that you are more successfully facing these archetypal fears than they are. Let us give you an example. The Zeta Reticuli have an ability to shift their focus from one body to another. Let us say you have a Zeta standing by a doorway and one leaning over an abductee. The one near the abductee can at will move his focus into the one who is standing at the door. During an abduction situation, the Zeta Reticuli have had the experience of spontaneously switching their focus from being the abductor to being the human abductee! It is instantaneous and it lasts only for a moment. But they get a taste of the type of fear that they've denied for quite some time.

If the focus becomes too uncomfortable for the Zeta during an abduction experience, they can switch the focus away from the one leaning over the abductee in order to avoid the experience?

Yes, exactly. The Zeta Reticuli are very good at avoidance. Yet they do not see it as avoidance in any way. They see it as *adaptation.*

Is the Zeta mass mind experiencing, in a sense, intrusion of its reality by us?

Yes. In previous chapters it was stated that you are visitors from within *them*. This is what we are referring to. These spontaneous and seemingly uncontrolled experiences they have regarding you are equal in intensity to the experiences that *you* have with *them*. It is shocking. It is frightening. And at this point it is not yet understood by them.

The Zeta Reticuli have rationalized that the shocks they experience when interacting with you are a product of *you* and the nature of your reality. They do not yet see any connection with themselves at this point concerning their own transformation.

One of the purposes of their being here is to experience these shocks and be transformed.

Exactly. Just as you are discovering the purpose of their interaction with you, they are in the process of discovering the ultimate purpose for your interaction with them.

Are they capable of speaking about this?

They are not aware of this at this time.

So it would do no good to ask them about their unexpected visions?

Correct. We would not suggest it at this time. It is premature. All that we have said so far is enough to assist individuals who are having contact to take the next natural step.

Is the visitor phenomenon occurring in areas that we don't suspect?

The contact phenomenon is coming to your world from many, many angles. Though there is denial, there is also integration. You are literally seeing it in nearly every phase of your development.

What is the reason for our denial?

151

One reason is the remembrance of the pain that extraterrestrial contact has caused you in your past—the fears of abandonment, the desire for salvation, the dysfunctional family systems that you were a part of with your forefathers. It is a desire to resist that experience in order to keep the pain away.

For this reason we have given an example of two different civilizations and the processes they went through in getting themselves ready for contact. Your civilization is a combination of the two, though you will also incorporate more individualistic qualities toward your acceptance of contact because of your sociological development.

We have also talked about how you as a terrestrial civilization are making first contact yourselves with another civilization—the Zeta Reticuli. It doesn't matter that they have come to you. You are opening contact with them by being who you are. You are initiating an intergalactic relationship by your agreement to interact with them. This agreement will continue. However, it will grow and change as you grow and change. Your evolution is intricately entwined.

10

Denial and Transformation

"This new stage we may be about to witness can be likened to the ending of an evolutionary childhood. . .It is time now for the Homo line to put away its childish things."
— Yatri from *Unknown Man: The Mysterious Birth of a New Species*

Imagine what it would be like if the abduction phenomenon was talked about openly. What would happen to our species if, on a large scale, we actually acknowledged our interactions with the visitors? What would happen to us if we deliberately sought to meet them in the daylight of our consciousness instead of the dark recesses of our minds?

Denial plays quite a profound role in our interactions with the visitors. The government denies their existence. The media ridicules the phenomenon. Individuals often choose to go through a personal hell rather than admit to loved ones that they have encountered the unknown. And most tragically, we often keep it even from ourselves.

Denial often shapes our lives because we must live in such a way as to keep the lie intact. As the denial increases, so does the personal pain. We have the power to heal this pain by taking full responsibility for not only the lie, but also that which the lie keeps hidden. Humans have the ability to take

153

full responsibility for the visitor phenomenon and consciously choose how it manifests in their lives.

In this chapter, Bashar addresses this human denial and how it can be used for personal and planetary transformation. He also discusses the future of the hybrid projects between the Zeta Reticuli and humans, as well as an overview of the visitor agenda for the 1990s and into the twenty-first century.

* * *

Bashar: We would like at this time to address your questions and comments regarding the interactions humans are having with the Zeta Reticuli. We wish to address the evolutionary ideas that the Zeta Reticuli present for you. We will take your questions.

What is the agreement that has allowed the current interactions between the visitors and humans to take place?

The agreement is a very ancient one. The agreement is on the part of several million souls. This agreement exists in order to achieve the completion of a specific genetic and spiritual evolution. This agreement spans not only your planet but the planets of your forefathers as well. This agreement is one that says, "At all costs, evolution will continue."

What type of evolution?

The type of evolution of which we speak is evolution that goes beyond any of your definitions at the present time. Evolution in its entirety encompasses the mental, emotional, spiritual and physical/genetic/etheric aspects of a species. This agreement spans time and space. It is an agreement that is not limited to your Earth plane.

Is a sense of urgency a part of this agreement?

Urgency denotes that there is a time limitation. In the very basic areas of the agreement there is no such understanding of limitation of time. However, instead of urgency, we would use the term compulsion.

Is this the type of agreement where something is being exchanged between two parties?

In your physical dimension, it *seems* as if there is an exchange between two separate parties (Zetas and humans). This translates as the Zetas receiving something from you, and you receiving something from them. That is simply one translation of the idea. In the very deepest sense of the agreement, there is no exchange per se, because those of you who made the agreement are playing out all of the roles in the scenario. Therefore you *all* get what you need.

So the nature of the agreement is a much more rich tapestry than we really suspect?

Yes. It cannot, in its entirety, be translated into your physical language. It is a compulsion. It is a drive that all species carry with them when they enter physicality. This drive or compulsion is also prevalent in nonphysical beings as well. It is that which drives all of us to continue expanding ourselves.

Recognize that you will only manifest the traumatic and dramatic fulfillment of your agreements when you deny the agreements themselves. If you chose to stop the denial, the way the agreement plays out would change.

So in this light, it is difficult to divide the agreement into two separate parties playing out two different aspects.

Ultimately, you cannot separate them. They are one and the same. For the sake of communicating these ideas, you may display the separation as symbolic and state that it is so.

Do the Zeta Reticuli feel that they have been invited here?

They do not *feel* they have been invited. They *know* they have been invited. *They are the invitation itself.*

Did we invite them?

You are the invitation itself as well. You did not extend an invitation from a place of not having invited them. You always have been the invitation itself by your nature, existence, agreements, and what you represent as a planetary species.

Then on a lower physiological level, the Reticulum could not have refused to come here? They must *come here?*

Correct.

With that foundation laid, why do we choose to invite them in the way we do?

At this point we would say, speaking loosely, it is not that you have necessarily chosen to experience it the way you do. What you have chosen instead is a *denied reality* of the agreement. This denied reality of the agreement is what dictates *how* the visitations manifest for you. Therefore, you have chosen to not yet remember the calls of evolution. You have chosen to not yet remember who you are and your relationship to other nonterrestrial beings. By those choices, you automatically choose that this interaction will occur in the realms of denial.

On another level, one could say that you have chosen it in this way to remind yourselves that you are in denial and that you have the opportunity to change that state of being. Drawing a situation into your reality, from which you must face your denial, will allow you to begin to remember.

Please answer this question only within the scope of what we are talking about. Why are we in this denial?

There are many levels to the answer. On the metaphysical level, it is the idea of not wanting to join with the Creator so you will not have to experience the pain of separating from the Creator again.

Another idea for this denial has to do with the purging of the very deepest layers of fear. You would not be able to access those fears to be purged if you did not first create an atmosphere of denial. Do you follow?

Yes. We are using denial as a specific tool to transform something very deep within our nature.

Exactly. On more superficial levels, the denial has to do with your unwillingness and fear of taking 100% responsibility for your reality and for that which you create. Therefore, you continue to give your responsibility to someone else and continue to play victim. This is an old, old pattern that cannot continue indefinitely. You are giving yourself the opportunity to purge that pattern.

So we are using the abduction scenario to deal with a general situation that the species has experienced for quite some time.

Yes. You are using the abduction situation (and other situations as well) to trigger your species' emotional evolution. However, the abduction situation is providing an enigma for you. Within this enigma is trauma. This will allow you then to face the unknown. You are *compelled* to face the unknown. In that unknown you will find many of your answers.

In respect to the visitors being the invited ones, what determines how the answer to the invitation will manifest?

The key factor will be the level of denial in which you engage yourselves. If you engage yourselves in a solid foundation of denial, that will dictate a certain type of experience with the visitors. That type of experience will take the shape of traumatic, otherworldly experiences because you refuse to create contact in your *conscious* reality. The less the denial, the more willingness you will have to face these situations in your waking, conscious state.

Recognize in your previous chapter that the culture known as Beta-4 manifested tremendous drama in their awakening because of their level of denial. That level of denial shaped and molded how the contact experience expressed itself in their society. It is the same with you. *Denial will be the key factor in molding how your visitation experiences occur in your reality.*

Will the nature of our invitation change?

The nature of the invitation will change only insofar as you are willing to consciously remove the veils and be willing to take responsibility for your own evolution individually and globally — and from that responsibility, seek out the unknown. Once you do that, the nature of the invitation *must* change because you will recognize it is not an invitation nor a compulsion. It becomes the dance of evolution, a movement, a spiral. You will recognize that movement and change represent existence itself.

And the Zetas' response to our perceived invitation will change also?

Yes.

Where are these encounters leading, and what will be the impact on the human consciousness?

At the present time, the human psyche is undergoing a tremendous amount of stress regarding these contacts. Even individuals who are not having contacts are vicariously feeling this stress because you are all linked together. This force that is created by these denied contacts is compelling you to face the unknown. This is compelling you to release the pressure in such a way that will provide you with relief. Relief can only come from facing that which is denied. You are moving toward a time when you much more openly and freely choose to confront that which you fear.

These contacts are allowing you a metamorphosis from the most physical levels of being to the most esoteric. It is truly a metamorphosis greater than you have seen on your world at any time previously. You are stepping into the next stage in your species evolution. The Zeta contacts are the magnet pulling you forward.

Will these encounters lead to personal transformation of something as basic as behavior patterns within a person?

The contacts on the individual level will absolutely lead to personal transformation. Personal transformation on a widespread level will then lead to species transformation.

This type of contact, which requires you to face the deepest, darkest fears within you, *must* change and break old behavior patterns. These contacts stimulate confrontation on the deepest levels of being. Once you confront these deep levels of being, you have no choice but to either lose yourself in that depth and despair or let the energy from the uncovering of those deep fears fuel you toward evolution. Some may choose to lose themselves in the depth and despair. That is their choice. That will be what they choose to play out. But for the most part, individuals will use the energy of that confrontation as fuel for their continued evolution.

Is there going to be a change in the public awareness of the visitors?

You are already beginning to see, as reflected in some of your media, that there has been a significant change regarding your perceived relationship with visitor beings. This will continue. You will find that the more you are willing to confront what they represent, the more your perceptions of them will be less of a caricature and more of real beings on equal level with you.

You will find that there will be a greater understanding of the psyche of the visitors as being entities who also seek evolution and fear annihilation as do you. You will begin to see the similarities between you, and in that compassion, understanding will dawn and cooperation will begin.

159

How are these encounters changing the Zeta Reticuli? Are they developing new ideas about themselves?

They are developing new ideas about themselves. Some of the new ideas are still somewhat frightening to them. They still see some of these new ideas as untested and therefore only hypotheses. However, with their curiosity and their desire for knowledge, any new idea that comes to them from their interactions with you will be engaged. They themselves are changing. They are growing. They are beginning to understand that even with their mass mind, they have segmented their consciousness in ways not too dissimilar from you. By watching you, they see their own fragmentation. By watching you, they learn to reawaken themselves.

So there may actually be something like a Zeta Reticuli subconscious? A mass-mind subconscious?

The word subconscious is not entirely accurate; however, the meaning you ascribe to it is. There is an aspect of their mass mind that has segmented itself and that is storing their hidden and denied aspects of who they are.

Would this manifest physically in the sense that there are some Zeta Reticuli-like groups who seem to be less evolved and out of communication with the other Zeta groups?

The lesser evolved and perhaps negative-oriented beings do represent externalized aspects of this denied reality. However, they exist of their own accord as well.

Do the Zeta Reticuli enter a kind of dream when they enter our mass consciousness and interact with us?

They are prone to entering a dreamlike state, an alternate subreality, if they allowed themselves to disconnect momentarily from their mass mind as they engage their curiosity in interacting with you as individuals. However, they very tightly control this possibility for fear of losing themselves.

Has this occurred?

Yes.

Would that account for some of the more bizarre interactions?

Most definitely.

Do they remember their experiences when they reestablish contact with their mass mind?

They do not remember it in exact terms as they have experienced it. It is dreamlike, and when they awaken into their mass-mind consciousness, it is as if they have had a very intense experience that is fraught with symbolism and archetypes that they do not understand.

Will this be occurring more frequently?

As they continue to deny the aspects they have repressed, it will continue. It must continue if they continue to deny. As they become more in touch with what they have sublimated, it will lessen.

Is there a meeting ground being constructed so we may be able to interact with them on a more intimate and direct level?

Yes, but you will first need to acknowledge each other and admit the reality of each other. That will be the time with which you can openly travel to the meeting ground and interact together.

Is that very far into the future?

It is beginning now for many of you as individuals. It may not be that far off.

So for us, that meeting ground is now our dreams.

Yes. Right now it is the only common ground.

Do the Zeta Reticuli dream?

They do not sleep, therefore they do not experience your definition of dreaming. However, when they *disconnect* from their mass-conscious mind, they experience something that can be likened to dreams. When you *connect* with the human mass mind, you experience the idea called dreaming. It is there the joint reality or the common ground occurs. There, you are both the mass mind and the individual as well as neither of them.

What is the next phase of contact with the visitors? What is the future of the genetic project?

The next phase of contact has already begun. The theme of this phase is the beginnings of equality. The qualities of this new phase of contact will become less traumatic as you begin to understand that you can initiate contact yourself. The nature of the contact will change as you begin to see your own versatility within the dynamic itself.

It is our perception that the year you call 1995 will be a significant time period for the beginnings of equal communication between you on a mass level. Contact may still occur in the dream state. It may still occur in quasi-physical realities, but the flavor of the contacts will change.

As for the genetic project, it is our understanding that very shortly upon your world will begin the birth of children physically who are beginning to carry genetic structures of the Zeta Reticuli adapted so that they can survive on Earth. Again, recognize that the babies born with these genetic structures do so by choice.

Will they use the genetics of those people for further experimentation and development of a hybrid species?

Yes. As these prehybrids are birthed, the experiential realities they interact with on Earth will trigger certain genetic codes that will provide the genetic material for the next stage in the genetic projects. This is a significant point in the genetic work because the genetics used from these prehybrid children will be obtained without force or trauma. These children will *voluntarily* be part of the experiments. This changes the energy of the experiments as a whole.

Will these children have a more conscious and intimate relationship with hybrids being developed?

Yes. The prehybrids will be able to give the Zetas valuable feedback and information on the psyche of the hybrids.

What is the significance of the hybrids to the Zeta Reticuli and the human race?

As the hybrids emerge, they represent an end to transformation through denial and herald an era of transformation through cooperation and conscious choice. That is one of the fundamental significant ideas that is part of the hybrid emergence.

On the physical level, the hybrid will represent a joining of two species at opposite ends of the scale, thus symbolizing an internal joining of polarity. It will become a willing cooperation in the process of integration and species transformation.

When will this new species appear?

As has been stated, you will begin to see the birthing very shortly (1994-1995) of children who are the prehybrids that will be the precursors to the later hybrid species. This birthing of the prehybrids, as we view it at the present time, will peak in number between January 1994 and March 1996. After that time period, a different phase will be activated. It is important to stress that the prehybrids and hybrids will not *replace* the human race, but instead add to its evolutionary diversification. That is all we can say now.

So the new hybrid species may come into existence in the twenty-first century?

Yes. Recognize that they are being created in many time continua. The time frames we speak to you about are only those relative to your Earth time continuum.

Speaking as one who represents a race birthed from humans and the Zeta Reticuli, we will emphasize that there is no failure or success of the genetic experiments. The genetic project continues, always has and always will, as an expression of the evolution of All That Is.

We would like to express our gratitude for what your race has chosen to manifest and for the gift that your race has given to all hybrid species — myself included. You have given a gift that will echo through time, a gift whose ripples will continually be felt for millennia. It is with this gratitude that we bid you joy in the confrontation of who you are and that which you will become.

* * *

The visitors exist as separate beings from ourselves. We are able to see them, touch them, and be touched *by* them. We can trace their history, learn about their psyche, and understand their motivations.

The visitors also exist within us; they are the shadows, the devas, the archetypes and fairies. They play out any available role in order to be perceived by us. Sometimes we have confused the role they play with who they really are. They are beings like ourselves, ever evolving, and just as lonely as we are. They too seek more of themselves.

Today in modern industrialized society there is no traditional structure to give meaningful form to the abduction experience. This has allowed for a painful alienation from one's peers and even from humanity itself. This condition may actually be beneficial to us, however. Now that our mystical traditions have all but disappeared, for the first time we may be able to see the visitors for what they really are. We are less able to clothe them in familiar costumes.

164

Since we live in a world of denial, they must come to us through our minds and our personal mythology. In this internal world there is no separation between us and them. We reflect each other. We are catalysts for each other. And most of all, it is here that we can learn to love each other and embrace the shadow within...and in so doing, learn to love ourselves.

11

Contactee Children

The bulk of the material in this book was originally channeled prior to its 1992 publication date. Since that time we have gathered more information. The following two chapters update the saga of the Visitors and their desperate desire to evolve beyond the limitations of their species.

The material in this chapter is derived from a channeling session held specifically for a group of children (and some adults) in Nevada who are contactees. The ages of the children range from very young (5 or 6) to 17 years old. There were approximately 13 children present with parents and other close friends. Many of the questions asked below were posed by the children in a further attempt to understand their contact experiences. This session was recorded in December 1993, well after the release of the first version of the book *Visitors from Within*.

Sasha: Before we take questions, we would like to make a brief comment about the children in your society who are now having contact. Many adults have done a lot of inner work to get to the point where they can face the contact they have had. The children who are now coming into your world are entering with more awareness and openness toward contact. This is quite significant for the entire human race.

Your children are the future of humanity. The awareness and understanding of your children regarding this phenomenon will always reflect where humanity is heading. The children here in this group tonight represent the hope for humanity. If your world evolves in the same direction these children are leading you to, you have nothing to worry about. They are paving the road to the future. This is a future that all of you would be proud and happy to live within.

Let us take this opportunity to thank the children for what they teach all of you. Thank you, children, for the gift you give to humanity. We are so very excited to talk with you.

Marsha: Sasha, this is Marsha. [Note: Marsha is the organizer of this children's support group]. *Your message hit me so hard because . . .* [she becomes emotional]

Your emotions are very centering.

Marsha: I have come to realize that the path we must take is through the children. We must teach them.

And you must let them teach you, too.

Marsha: I have a group of about 13 kids who come to this contact support group . . . I think I am answering my own question! I guess it is all perfect.

It is. We thank you for your service. This service is filling a void in your society much more than you realize. Thank you!

In working with children, adults touch the inner child as well. That is so very important. As we have discussed in the past, many of the blockages kept in the adult consciousness come from childhood. As you work with children, you also work with the child within each adult. Do not underestimate the significance of that idea.

All of you have been given a gift this night with the children here, with Marsha's love and support and with each other. Recognize that the beauty, joy and love that you see within these children must exist within yourselves or you could not perceive it. It exists within *all* of you.

Child: Do blind people get visited?

Very interesting question! Yes they do, but the interpretation of the visitation experience is different, especially if the person has been blind since birth. He/she is then very comfortable with his/her inner reality in a way that those with sight may not be. So the visitations that are made with those people blind from birth have less separation inherent in them than the contacts that happen with people who have sight.

The inner world is much more homogeneous and cohesive for one who is blind. This is because physical reality for sighted people is dominant and helps to create separation.

If any of you wish to do an experiment and perform a well-known shamanic ritual, let us suggest the following: Take three days outside of your normal activities and have someone there with you. Cover your eyes for three days. During those three days, get in touch with your new sensory abilities, not only sound, touch and smell, but your psychic senses as well. You will find that if within those three days you have any contact experiences, they will have a different flavor. This is a wonderful initiatory experience, very similar to some shamanic training given in some cultures around your world.

Parent: Are there things that I can do to better help my children further their contact experiences? How can I help them grow faster?

Are you perceiving that they are having difficulty with their encounters?

Parent: No, not at the moment.

The greatest gift you can give them to help their own evolution is to continue to engage them in dialogue about their experiences so they can feel, on a very deep level, that their experiences are part of a valid reality. What are the ages of your children?

Parent: *Fourteen and ten.*

If they are willing, you can have creative sessions where they may want to do artwork or some type of creative expression where they can channel their energy of contact into this physical reality with you. An example might be drawing a picture with an ET theme. This will help dissolve the boundaries between the levels of their consciousness so they can begin integrating their experiences into their daily lives. As you help them do this, they will accelerate quite rapidly. So will you! Be prepared!

Child: *How old are you?*

In Earth terms, I am approximately 34, which is a baby in my society! My lifespan can be anywhere from 200 to 500 years. I am relatively very young, though an adult.

Child: *I had a dream one time. It seemed like it was more in the future, around 1998. My mom and brother were in the dream. We were standing in front of a building. About four teenagers came up to us and asked us if we were going to go see the mothership. It was about 3:00 a.m. They were waiting for us. We said no, that we were not going to go. They left. Then it was daylight and we were in front of a 7-11. We were looking up in the sky and there were Air Force planes flying in a perfect triangular formation. They were having dogfights with civilian helicopters with guns on them, all the while staying in perfect formation. Then we saw a mountain. There was a crevice in the mountain. A big, round mothership started coming up from the crevice. Could you explain anything about this?*

To a degree, some of the dream is literal. You did have an encounter that night, though the actual memory was not recalled clearly in the dream. That night you were given information about the next eight years or so (1994-2002) and about what will happen with the UFO situation in your world. What you remembered in the dream is symbolic of the information you were given that night by the ETs who were communicating with you. First you were shown that there were various Earth crafts (fighter planes or helicopters) that were flying, yet fighting each other, both civilian and military. This represents the idea that in the next eight years or so there will still be power struggles between civilians, the shadow government and the military about the ET information. Your dream was a symbolic representation of that idea.

After that, the ship in your dream came from the crevice in the mountain. Symbolically this means that after the power struggle ends, the knowledge of the ET connection to Earth will eventually be known and revealed to humanity. Because the ship was coming from a crevice in the Earth and outward into the sky, it is symbolic of a release from the subconscious or hidden areas out into the open. Basically, there will be some fighting primarily between the three factions listed previously, but eventually the information will be brought out into the open. This is the basic translation of the information given to you that night.

Parent: Keith was talking about how important it is to take care of the dysfunction and issues that we have from this life so that we can release those blocks. He said that how we perceive contact is influenced by our family history.

Yes. Basically, all contact experiences are interpreted through your belief systems. Your belief systems are formed by (1) past-life experiences, (2) present-life childhood experiences, and (3) how you dealt with these experiences from childhood to the present. We call these belief systems *data blocks*. They are what make up your conscious mind and belief systems. If they are very rigid and there is a lot of pain or anger held there from childhood, your contact experiences will activate those unresolved emotions. The reaction that you then have to contact will not necessarily be because of the contact itself, but instead will be a reaction to the dysfunctional aspects within yourself that the contact has triggered. So the more and more you work within yourself to clear out your fears and unresolved issues to make yourself a stronger and more empowered person in the present time, the more balanced and real your contact interpretations will be.

Many contactees have already done this work because they have gotten through most of the terror and fear with which other contactees are still struggling. You will find that the more you are willing to achieve a sense of empowerment and strength within you, the more your contact experience will change. Your contact experiences *must* change as you change. They will become even more enriching and profound than they already are.

Parent: In talking about family systems, I think there are several of us here who have no recall prior to the age of five. Can you explain why that is so?

This is different for each person, but let us explore some possibilities. First, for a good many people on your world, you do not "lock in" to this reality until you are approximately five years old. Prior to age five, you are in and out and experiencing several realities at once.

Many of you who remember childhood contact experiences will remember a significant contact experience around the age of five. This is because the contact is a trigger point when your higher self is asked, "These are the agreements you've made for this life. Do you want to stay on Earth?" For many of you who are contactees, there is usually an opportunity around the age of five to either commit to this reality or "exchange" soul energy with another consciousness who wishes to be here.

The age of five is targeted for several reasons. For most people, age five is when formal schooling begins. In a sense, you then become initiated into this reality, deprogrammed from the soul's perspective of reality and programmed into the Earth perspective. You have gotten a taste of Earth reality and are given an opportunity to decide whether you still wish to be of service. Sometimes the soul really wanted only those first five years of experience.

Sometimes souls who will later incarnate as Zeta-human hybrids will experience those first five years of life and then depart in order to understand the Earth experience before the programming sets in.

Child: I would like to know if you can help me with an embarrassing fear. I'm afraid of the dark.

One who is afraid of the dark can cut through all of the surface issues and go straight to the heart by being very willing to find the darkness within. All of the shadows, inner demons and negative archetypes that lie deep within the consciousness must be faced squarely. When they are, a fear of the dark will no longer be present. The fear is there only as a reminder of what is going on inside you. So how does one face this inner darkness?

There are many different ways to confront this kind of fear. You may use traditional therapy such as Jungian therapy. Any methodology that will allow you to go within and pull up the dark voices and befriend them will help considerably. There is a belief inside you that something in the dark is going to annihilate you.

Child: I know what that is, but . . . my conscious mind wants to stop this stupid behavior. My subconscious puts on the brakes every time I try.

We understand. If you are not having success in stopping the behavior in the physical world, release your need to do so. Let yourself be afraid of the dark! That, in and of itself, is facing darkness. It is extremely empowering. Let yourself *feel* the fear. Don't resist it. Resisting the fear is actually, in a sense, taking you further away from feeling it. Let yourself be afraid.

Child: That's not a problem!

Good! Now, this time don't feel bad or guilty because of the fear.

Keith: One of the main blockages you are experiencing is not the fear, but the judgment of the fear. Fear won't block you, but judgment will. There is a long history of a certain type of fear in the human race that you are also experiencing. Think of an owl about to pounce on a mouse. Do you think the mouse fears the dark? Yes! Because it is being preyed upon in darkness. One of the primary screen memories of the Zetas is the owl. It is a predator from the sky that comes and snatches you in the night.

You are also experiencing a primal fear, a genetic fear of the dark. There is nothing wrong with that.

This genetic fear probably goes back to the genetic evolution of all species of animals. Remember, our primate ancestors were snatched and reengineered into Homo sapiens. The Neanderthals had a tremendous fear of being preyed on in the night. Imagine the terror of being primitive man in ancient days and seeing some strange evolution occurring not only in your body but in your consciousness. A tremendous fear was felt then. You are about to change genetically yet again. Whether or not each human is consciously being altered genetically now, we are all experiencing tremendous changes in our consciousness. We are becoming a new species now, just as our primitive human ancestors became a new species in the past.

Sasha: Recognize that all evolution is cyclical. You are now experiencing the same thing as your ancestors did. When this cycle began, humankind was primitive. Primitive humans were "abducted." These primitive humans were genetically altered and allowed to advance to the next level of being. Now Homo sapiens is being advanced yet again. You are, in a sense, ending the cycle with the same pattern as your ancestors. Once again abductions are happening, and this is bringing up the old species memory of abduction. This time you are closing a cycle and moving once again into a new cycle of evolution. You are reexperiencing an ancient trauma that is being activated in present time.

At the same time that all abductees are healing the fear and trauma on an individual level, the fear and trauma felt by the human species for hundreds of thousands of years is being healed as well. This is why it feels like such a huge weight to carry. It feels larger than you. The healing will traverse generations and eons.

There is one who wishes to speak now. We will have to assist this entity, for he has not spoken through a human before. This entity is a Zeta-human hybrid. He is equivalent in human counting to approximately eleven years of age. The Zetas have had a difficulty in lengthening the lifespan of many of the hybrids. They often die or transition at what you would call physiological puberty. This male is about to enter that life stage, which is a very vulnerable stage for a hybrid. The Zetas working with him do not know whether he will make it.

He has agreed to offer this communication. We do not know how it will come through, so we will ask for your assistance. [Pause]

Hybrid: Your reality is dark . . . darkness.

Keith: Do you feel the channel's body?

Yes. I am in a glove. I cannot see you. Where are you?

Keith: That's okay. Don't try to see us right now. Do you have a name by which you wish to be referred for this communication? A sound?

. . . Ethil. Ethil.

Keith: Where did you just come from, Ethil? Where is your body now?

In the replication room.

Keith: Are there others with you?

Yes. Others of my kind. I feel energy in motion [emotion]. My human facilitators tell me it is called fear. I must pass through this transition. I must succeed. I must succeed.

Keith: What do you fear?

Noncompletion, termination. I must succeed. I must give this gift. Do you understand?

Keith: Yes. We all terminate.

There is an urgency, there is a need. I must complete.

Keith: The message of the Essassani to you is this: "The project worked. It has been completed. It will be successful."

But I must succeed!

Keith: You will succeed. You are speaking to us now. You are succeeding.

I speak in darkness. I chose to give a gift to my Fathers and to my grandchildren, and I must give this gift! I do not know how to communicate this.

Keith: *We will receive the gift. We accept the gift. Would you like to speak to the others?*

Are you not all of them?

Keith: *No. I am only me, a singular being.*

A singular physiological unit?

Keith: *Yes. I am me, totally me. There are others who are themselves. They will speak to you differently than I do. Would anyone else like to ask questions?*

Members of the audience: *How can we help you to succeed? Is there anything we can do?*

Please come to us and take us over the threshold. Please reach to us. Please help us. I do not know how to tell you to do this, but come to us!

Member: *I will come to you anytime the Elders say it is all right. We all will.*

Please do not be afraid of us. We look strange.

Member: *You look beautiful! In my eyes you are beautiful. I will come to you anytime. I've called out to you.*

I have this vision. This is a ritual that I have been taught by my Fathers. If we all hold hands and walk across the threshold together, we will become. Do you understand?

Audience: *Yes! Yes, yes.* [The group holds hands with Ethil.]

In your receptive state, your fragmented "rest time," please come to us and help us over the threshold. Please. All the levels of importance have not been communicated to you, but you, my Fathers and we all need this joining. Wish it, and come to us. We will make the leap together. We will succeed. Do you understand?

[Various responses.] *Yes. Very much. We will be there. You have our word. Together we can do it.*

[The group holds hands in a circle with Ethil. There is much emotion in the room. There is a pause.]

I just felt! My Fathers have taught us that this holding of hands and the feeling of One People is the way they celebrate their communion. When they teach us this, we feel a quickening in the chest. I felt this from you! You have given a gift. I will share it. How may we thank you?

Member: *By succeeding in your desire.*

With your assistance. [Communication ended].

* * *

We never followed up on this 1993 encounter with Ethil until five years later, at the end of 1998. We had no idea of the impact our group had on Ethil and his people. In 1998 Ethil spoke to us again and revealed the profound evolution he and his people made because of the intent and love of this small group of children and adults in Nevada. Because of this interaction, Ethil's people began to gain confidence and strength even amidst their confusing evolutionary challenges. The leap that Ethil and his people made is one that gives hope for the future evolution of all species everywhere.

12

Heart of the Children

We need to learn how to square the circle - to regain childhood's capacity for joy while preserving the knowledge and wisdom that we have gained as adults.

- Whitley Strieber from *The Secret School: Preparation for Contact*

Intrigued by the session with the children in 1993, we recently inquired about Ethil and whether or not he survived through puberty. Nearly five years after the original session for the children, Keith Priest and Ron Holt (Lyssa's husband) questioned Sasha about the hybrid project. What follows is an excerpt from that session. To our surprise, some startling information was revealed.

Sasha: There is another entity that wishes to speak who is overshadowing us. Let us first introduce him. The entity you spoke to five years ago called Ethil did, in fact, survive puberty, and he now speaks to you from a time continuum very far in the future from that 1993 communiqué. Please understand that your continuum and his do not line up. He speaks to you from the point of view of an elder. He is considered an elder among his people because he was among the first of the hybrids to survive past puberty. Are you ready to speak to him? [Sasha pauses.]

Ethil: It has been quite a journey. To you it may seem like just a few short planetary cycles, but much time has passed in my life. I would like to tell you as much as I can about what has transpired in this genetic project from my point of view. Then you will be free to ask questions.

I can truly say that it is difficult to even know where to start. I am a very different being from the one to whom you spoke cycles ago. The transition from childhood through puberty was at times a difficult one. I did take on some of the infection problems that others before me had experienced and nearly lost my corporeal life. I do not know why or how, but guidance of a sort that I did not understand took me through the process of life as if I were walking through a tunnel and came out the other side. At the time I did not know what this guidance was.

As I lay in my bed, very often in pain, I wondered if the species I was helping to birth would ever survive. I knew that the key to survival was in the encounters between humans and hybrid entities. In the [first edition of *Visitors from Within*], you discussed the idea of humans holding or nurturing hybrid babies, did you not? [Yes.] At that time, the knowledge of the human-hybrid connection was in its infancy. Later, as the project developed, the relationships between the humans (especially the children) and the hybrids became essential to our survival.

The guidance I received was insistent, so I followed it. I asked my caregivers to find human children who would be willing to assist me and others who were ill, as I was. Some of the children who agreed to assist me were in the 1993 group. If you remember, when I first spoke to them I was very young. Some of these children came and sat with me as I lay ill. At first we did not know what we were supposed to do together. We decided we would simply interact and see where that took us. We found that the nature of communication between human children and the hybrids was different than communication between human adults and hybrids, because there is still much fear on the part of human adults. But with human children, there is much less fear.

180

The interaction between the children and the hybrids was one from the heart. The connection between our species was made through the heart by way of the children. This was the missing element. Once the connection between our species became stronger, other children volunteered. Some loud voices on your world will tell you that our interactions with you are of fear, and that they are something to be terrified of. They tell you that our interactions are evil, but the voices of thousands of people who are having beautiful and loving experiences with us are never heard. Those people who so deeply love us began to consciously step forward, and they helped us activate the love within us. The type of love experienced by my species (Zeta-human hybrid) is very different from the Zetas' love. This love strengthened our immune systems so that we were able to fight the infections. It also eased the hormonal changes we experienced as we entered puberty. The puberty experience was not primarily a hormonal change, but a change of heart energy, which regulated the hormonal system. It balanced it very well.

It was successful enough for me to be able to speak to you now from what seems very distant from the beginnings of the project. In your way of viewing time, I am now very old. Those who came after me survived, for the most part.

You who are familiar with cosmology will remember that the race you know as Essassani (the home species of the notorious entity Bashar) is comprised of human and Zeta DNA. Hybrids evolve into and eventually become Essassani. My genotype is a precursor to that which you call Essassani. We are not yet Essassani; we are their predecessors.

Keith: *Are you able to have children now with each other?*

It is hit or miss. Sometimes it happens, sometimes it does not. If we wish to breed, it is much more successful when done in the laboratory. We are fertile in that we produce fertile eggs and sperm. We remind you that this fertility is because of the evolution of our hearts. The heart of humanity and the heart of the Zetas had to integrate because they were polar opposites. The Zeta race (my Fathers) represents the opposite polarity of the human race (my Mothers). For humans to interact with Zetas, they must see their opposite self, go into the void, and walk through their fears.

Ron: When the children and adults were holding your hand in the 1993 session, what did you feel? What happened?

That moment of unification created what might be called a vortex. It was my first experience of love as humans understand it. It was being given to the other hybrids and me from such a place of unconditionality that its purity traversed the dimensions and *literally* created an alchemical process within my genetic structure.

Ron: So this also created a new time line or probability through the advent of the vortex of unconditional love? Did this actually create a future in which you could survive?

It was that moment which created a new continuum for the Essassani race to eventually evolve. With respect to the adults who were present, this continuum had to be created for us by the children, not by the adults. This is because the essence of the Essassani is infinitely childlike — not childish, but childlike. The children had to do this. Children cannot biologically lend their eggs and sperm as adults do, but they gave us something equally important.

Ron: Just moments before the touching of hands between you and the children, were you still of a hive mind?

Recognize that I am a hybrid, not a Zeta. I was raised primarily in a hive environment, but was consistently exposed to individualized consciousness in the form of humans.

Ron: In touching hands, did you change from more of a hive orientation to an individualized one? By feeling the vortex of the heart come alive inside you, did it create a personal reference point? Was love experienced differently?

We did not move from hive consciousness to the polarity of individualized consciousness, but rather to the center point between both. We moved to the point of paradox where both exist in harmony.

Keith: Let me point out something interesting. In Chinese medicine, the fire points of the heart and pericardium channel are in the palm. Thus holding hands would activate the heart. The Zetas experience heart connections through their palms, and so do children. In Oriental medicine and the five elements, kidney energy (or sexuality) destroys heart energy, so at puberty the heart struggles against sexuality and is destroyed by kidney, which is actually a more powerful organ physiologically than the heart.

So humans spend their adult life trying to integrate their hearts with their sexuality. Hmm.

Keith: And they usually don't do such a good job in terms of their spiritual evolution because the kidneys (sexuality) are so powerful. Keep in mind that the kidneys also govern fear; fear and sexuality come from the kidneys. So it is important to reach one's inner humanity before puberty in order to make that heart connection. I'm not talking about individuals; I am talking more in a general sense in terms of our population.

Of course, we have part of your physiological structure and we do carry much of your meridian system. That event in 1993 when we held hands with the children and adults changed our future forever.

Ron: Were there more interactions with humans after you reached puberty?

Yes, mostly with children, but some adults as well. We attempted some experiments to activate the heart in adult humans the way it was done to us so they could experience the same type of integration that we did. It was successful to some degree; however, there is such a difference in our environment and yours that the shift for humans became uncomfortable. The success came in a form you call spiritual revelation.

Keith: So where have you spent most of your life?

Reality is so very different for my people. I have spent most of my life in flux between continua. I have also spent some of my life on a planet that was being terraformed. This planet is also a precursor to Essassani. It will not become Essassani, but it is its precursor.

Keith: *Have you ever had any adventures?*

Every moment is an adventure!

Keith: *No, I mean going off on your own somewhere. Did you ever build your own ship?*

That is not really a focus for me in this life.

Keith: *So you never had that individual urge to strike out on your own?*

No. The way my species expresses individuality right now might be considered limited when viewed from the human mind. Please do not demean our expressions of individuality. We express individuality right now by getting ideas and acting on them—usually in the context of an interaction with humans or another species. This is something, of course, that my Fathers (Zetas) have never done. They do not receive individual ideas; instead, they get collective revelations.

Ron: *Following the 1993 contact with the children, it must have been quite apparent what had taken place. There must have been evidence of change. Were others aware of your personal contact with the human children?*

It was part of the experiment. We must say that oftentimes our Fathers get desperate, though they will not admit it. It was a desperate attempt to create some form of shift in what seemed to be our certain demise. Our Fathers calculated that at the rate we were deteriorating, we would soon die out. In understanding this, they often performed acts of desperation, but are unlikely to admit it. (These acts of desperation are collectively decided upon.)

Keith: *So they reached out to the humans and were put in proximity to the humans in order to experience what they did.*

Yes.

Ron: What did the Zetas think you would gain by taking this desperate step?

At that time they could not logically conceive of a positive outcome. The rationale was more along the lines of sticking a finger in a light socket to get a shock. This shock would reset the system or, as you say, reboot the computer. There was only a sense or intuition that the act would produce a reboot. They could not, however, conceive of the nature of that reboot.

Ron: Did they understand what properties of the experience caused your recovery?

Even now they do not fully understand it. My people understand it, though. My Fathers attempt to understand it through their own rigid belief system. They are trying. They know it works, but they do not know why.

Ron: After you showed signs of success, did they immediately begin bringing other hybrids through the same process?

Yes, they did. But if you knew my beloved Fathers, you would know that they test things to death. They study things to death. (You can see that we are learning your human sayings!) Even though they continued the heart-activation process, they were testing it from every conceivable angle in order to understand it.

Ron: Do your Fathers still exist? [Yes.] *I don't know if you can speak for them, but do they see that in their own genetic line it was as far as they could progress? Do they see that a change must take place?*

They clearly see it, yes. But they could not conceive of what that change would entail.

Ron: I salute you for your pioneering spirit. The human spirit is built on that pioneering attitude. I salute your willingness to surrender to the greater process by coming through the other side and birthing into a new reality.

Then you honor my human Mothers, for it is from them that we have gained these qualities.

Let me attempt to express the idea of a continuum for a moment. This is a difficult concept for linear-thinking humans to grasp (no disrespect intended). Though I can speak to you now from my continuum (which is far in the future from the Ethil who spoke to you in 1993), this does not mean that my Fathers are not still visiting you or that there are not other interactions between my Fathers and humans still occurring with humans who have not made the transition from fear to love. All continua exist and interact with you simultaneously. In order for you as a human to change which continuum you interact with, you must first change yourself. The more into fear you are (which occurs early on in the visitation experience), the less evolved continuum will be the one you visit. As you evolve from fear to love and expand your belief systems and horizons, you move more fully into the heart and can see with the higher vision. You then begin interacting with the more evolved continuum. It is entirely up to you. *You* are responsible for choosing the continuum with which you will interact through who you are as a person and through your own spiritual evolution.

This does not mean that if you are still experiencing the phenomenon from a place of fear, you are bad or not spiritual enough. It simply means that it is something you still need to learn for your own growth. It is something that will benefit you tremendously should you engage the process. It is important to state that. All beings and all consciousness evolve.

Keith: *Are you involved in the so-called abductions?*

No, not directly. We interact primarily with willing children. That is my number-one activity.

Ron: *How many hybrids are there? Have many made it in your continuum?*

There are approximately seven to eight thousand.

Ron: Are you evolved both technologically and emotionally, or have you let go of technology altogether?

In our continuum there really isn't a difference between technology and spirituality because they have blended so much. You might look at us and think we are godlike and therefore more evolved. We simply are who we are. We manifest our isness in whatever way is appropriate. We know that is a very vague answer, but it is the only one that makes sense to us.

Keith: Have you ever done anything that didn't make sense to you?

I never take the time to think about whether things make sense. My actions and I are the same thing. My actions are me, so I do not ask whether or not I make sense.

Keith: Coming from a Zeta background, your actions are heavily embedded in your perceived logic, and Zetas would not do anything that didn't make sense to them.

With respect to my Fathers, my race is more imaginative. We get that from our Mothers. However, from my point of view there is nothing I could do that would be outside myself.

Keith: That's a typical Zeta response, though! [Laughter.]

You humans do not realize that anything you do is still you. There is no such thing as something that is not of you.

Keith: That is true, but when you are totally enlightened on a matter, you lose the valuable impact and catalyst of that experience. It is the lack of awareness (the spot in the shadow) that allows a unique catalyst to come about.

We do not have that form of separation as our Mothers do. However, we are still capable of experiencing what you call surprise from time to time. We do not experience it as often as our Mothers do.

Ron: After the meeting with the Earth children when things started to change and an evolution of the heart began happening, did you find any conflicts between your heart and intellect? Was there an intellectual dilemma because of your new spontaneous emotional capabilities?

I spoke earlier about the unseen guidance I received to connect with the children. Somehow I did not question it. I felt its urgency and followed it. That was not a big challenge for my people. Is that what you meant?

Ron: In a sense. Here in the human condition, many of us have conflicting motivations. Sometimes our motivations come from logic and reason, sometimes from emotion. At times we find ourselves in a paradox, juggling the two. Sometimes the heart wins, sometimes the head. In this dance between the two, we find an interesting compromise where a greater part of ourselves can step in and balance the conflict. Did you go through a similar evolution as you went from childhood to adulthood?

No. We did not have that separation within our consciousness, because our shift manifested through an alchemical process.

We are not yet an established species. The continuum we reside within traverses several densities and dimensions. We will not fully anchor in a density or dimension until we become an established species. The established species will become the Essassani.

The kind of shift that we experienced is much more difficult if the species is already established, with centuries of patterns and habits. Since we were a new life form being born, we were able to start with a clean slate, so to speak.

Keith: So is history itself encoded in the DNA? Is DNA, in a sense, composed of history? And must it be selectively removed from humans?

My Fathers and other species have previously said to you that genetic engineering on a cosmic scale *is* natural evolution.

Keith: So when we transform and evolve, we are transforming our DNA, correct? [Yes.] *And then we are transforming our history as well, correct?* [Yes.] *So when we become something new, we no longer have the same history.*

In that sense, yes.

Keith: So the memories of history must be transformed, and they are overlaid on the DNA?

Yes!

Ron: But we would have a tie, or a leash, to that which we were.

Keith: Is that why it is so difficult to change?

Yes, and this is why many of your forefathers have attempted to create a new species (altering the DNA and thus species history) in order to make profound leaps in evolution. Please understand the perspective from which we speak. Species evolution is not on the shoulders of one person. The entire process is holographic. Whatever one person does assists the whole.

This information we have given about the children will be significant for many people reading this book. Parents reading these words will know without a shadow of a doubt that their child is one of those to whom we are referring. To those parents we will say not to doubt it. It is a gift we cherish forever.

Keith: Do you continue to communicate with the children who were present in the 1993 session?

Yes. About 70% of them are still in communication with us through their own free will. Some of it is conscious, some of it is not. This communication will be maintained throughout their life as long as they wish it. They are my family.

Keith: So from your future perspective, did these children ever meet with you physically?

Physically, no. That is because of the nature of my reality. I am transdimensional at this point. It is very difficult for a human to hold that type of experience. From my future perspective these children do not remember our contacts in the same way they would remember meeting someone on the street. They remember me as a thread of strength and beauty that ran through their lives.

Keith: *Do you live long enough to meet some of your future species (Essassani) coming back in time?*

At this point they are not yet allowed to meet with us.

Keith: *Because your formation is not complete?*

Yes, and because it would be the same idea as your meeting face to face with your forefathers. It is an alchemical process to which they are not yet willing to submit us. We honor their wisdom on this subject.

We would like to thank both of you for allowing us to complete a cycle that we began in your 1993 time period. It has closed a door, yet opened another one. It has been very important that we express the significance of the role of the children. We are not just speaking about the children we spoke to in 1993, but all children on Earth who are the seedlings of the future and who will build the continuum that all of you are to walk for all time. These seedlings are the hope and the future. They have given us our future. For that we will be eternally grateful.

Now we will take our leave and Sasha will speak with you. Once again, it has been an honor.

* * *

Sasha: Thank you, Ron and Keith, for your support. Are there any further questions?

Ron: *Were you personally assisting in this alchemical process that Ethil described?*

In 1993 we were facilitating the energetic meeting between the humans and Ethil. The entity Bashar also assists from time to time in situations such as this. Prior to 1993 Bashar, Harone and myself often worked as a triad in this process.

Keith: *Obviously the Zetas are not truly alien to humanity. There has to be a deep connection that brings the two species together. It is a reunification of something in a unique way to create something new. I would go so far as to say that those who* *had a hand in engineering the humans also had a hand in engineering the Zetas. How else could it be?*

Yes, that race would be called the Founders, and you discussed them in your book *The Prism of Lyra*. We would also like to bring up an issue that has been debated many times in your past about who, exactly, the Zetas are. In *Visitors from Within* the Apexians were discussed as being the species who became the Zetas. It has also been debated by others that the Zetas are really humans coming from the future to influence yourselves.

Keith: Considering the nature of time and space, couldn't it be both?

Absolutely yes! Many people would feel that they need a definitive, either/or answer. Are the Zetas Apexians (a race outside of yourselves) or are they future humans — a literal aspect of yourselves returning to heal its past and change its future? It does *not* have to be one or the other. In fact, because reality is cyclical and not linear, a definitive answer does not make sense. It is both! Therein lies the paradox. As we have said many times, when one approaches a paradox, one is the closest to the truth.

Keith: I have an image in my mind I would like to explore. We have a model called space and a model called time. When we put them together we call that space/time. There is something in between the two that, through the alchemy between the Zetas and humans, will bring about a new reality.

Yes. When you have two polarities, you will continue to remain in a polarized universe as long as you simply bounce back and forth between the two. However, the true understanding of whether or not you are truly integrating polarities will come if you experience paradox. If you are experiencing paradox, it is a good sign that two polarities are being alchemically integrated and creating a third idea. You will not complete that integration or that alchemical change if you do not experience paradox.

Right now, when you bandy about the idea of whether the Zetas are you or whether they are Apexians, you are now dancing in a realm of paradox. This means that you are indeed integrating and beginning to create an alchemical change. You do not have to have an answer now; you will need to simply continue to dance in the realm of paradox, because all will eventually be revealed. This is not a yes or no answer because this is not a yes/no universe.

All the hypothesizing in the world will not make you see anything clearly. You must walk through the door of experience. Another insight into why the alchemical process with the children happened is because children do not have a problem experiencing paradox.

Let us discuss what is happening with the Zeta contact experience in your 1998/1999 continuum. As Ethil said, there is a whole spectrum of experience from the fear-based to the love-based and everything in between. That spectrum of contact is still present on Earth now. Individuals are still having fear-based experiences as well as love-based ones. However, a great majority of individuals who were having fear-based experiences in the 1980s and '90s have moved themselves through the spectrum and are now moving into love-based experiences. The nature of their contacts is changing. A new set of people are now moving into the awareness of having contact, and they are also beginning to move from fear to love. It is an evolutionary process; it is a species evolution.

Ultimately, moving from fear to love is an idea that nearly everyone will need to experience at one time or another. This movement from fear to love will be experienced whether it is through Zeta interactions or other means.

Something that wasn't addressed in the original material for this book (which was channeled in the late 1980s and early 1990s) has to do with the different factions of Zetas and/or humans who are conducting various contact activities. Each of these groups has a different agenda. We are not going to explore this idea in depth here because this book does not explore who is doing what to whom. This book explores the nature of the species evolution that is occurring through these interactions.

We will say, however, that there are bona fide ET/human interactions happening. Humans are also having contact experiences that are not based on visitations by real extraterrestrials. These experiences have more to do with covert paramilitary and secret government agendas as well as cult-based activity. These "contacts" disguise themselves as extraterrestrial activity to confuse the issue. Just about every scenario you can think of is being explored on Earth at this time, and for a variety of reasons. The experience a given person has depends on the choices he/she makes and on his/her life's purpose.

Once again let us stress that you change the experience by changing who you are. You change the experience by becoming more of your true self. This includes becoming more empowered, more heart-centered and spiritually connected with yourself and calling your internal fragments back home. As you do this, you become more integrated, and the alchemical process of transformation occurs. You then move yourself into a new frequency reality where your contacts *must* change. This is an essential point to stress.

It is our wish that individuals do not get caught up in who is doing what to whom and why. Don't be distracted by the mindset that says, "This group is the good guys" and "That group is the bad guys." That mindset will keep you polarized. Quite frankly, the universe is not so conveniently organized. Do not look outside yourselves for the answers. These polarity judgments (good and bad) are just a dramatic distraction that takes you away from yourself and your evolution.

Your natural spiritual evolution will remove you from this distracting drama and move you back into the heart. That is the essential key to transformation. You are moving from mind to heart, from physical to spiritual. The ET contact scenarios on your world are a way to stimulate this evolution. Do not be distracted by gloom and doom and drama. Go within, and all the answers you need will be there when you commit to yourself to becoming your unlimited potential. The doors of contact open in a very different way when you make that commitment. Those doors never lead down a road of fear. They take you home to yourself.

Epilogue

"The whole Progress of Nature is so gradual, that the entire Chasm from a Plant to Man, is filled up with divers[e] Kinds of Creatures, rising one above another, by so gentle an Ascent that the Transitions from one Species to another are almost insensible...is it not probable there are more Species of Creatures above than beneath us?"

—John Wesley, 1770

Long ago when ancient man began to be replaced by the stronger and more intelligent *Homo sapiens*, a deep, archetypal fear welled up within the collective soul of this ancient man. He knew his time was short. He knew the end was near. His primal being screamed out with the fear of annihilation. Yet this primal being relinquished its hold on the human collective soul. A new dawn broke upon the horizon of humankind.

One can only intuitively know that he is infinitely evolving. In the midst of this evolution, it is often difficult to see beyond the current experience into the expanse of the unknown. But there is indeed one constant in the universe—evolution. It is a tide that both physical and nonphysical beings cannot resist. The undertow of this tide is great; often it leaves beings gasping, unsure of their next steps. But ultimately the tide creates waves that carry all beings to the shore of their destiny.

Humans upon the Earth are in the midst of an evolutionary leap. While we are riding this wave, we cannot perceive it in its totality; hence, most are unaware of its massive force. But being unaware does not change the fact that it is occurring. No stone will be left unturned. The tide of evolution is washing over humans physically, mentally, emotionally, and spiritually. It is at times both subtle and blatant. It can bathe us in the serenity of warm and temperate waters. Or the piercingly cold water can take our breath away.

Are humans alone, enduring this species transformation in quiet solitude? Fortunately not. For it is not just humans on this small planet Earth who are transforming. Humans are part of a vast galactic network. When one portion of this network transforms, so does the network itself. Creation is a never-ending interlocking puzzle, with the picture constantly changing.

So who are these others transforming with humans? To most, they are shadows, dream images, devas, and archetypes. They are all those, yes. But they are also sentient beings, some physical like ourselves. The claxon is sounding for all to hear. We all hear the same call of evolution.

In this book we have explored several issues that many humans fear. Archetypally we have created external forces to send us the messages about human evolution. These messages manifest as extraterrestrial beings—either benevolent or malevolent in nature. Yes, these beings exist independently of humans. They too are evolving. Yet many of them understand the interconnectedness of all creation, and they think we do as well. They are watching...waiting. Like ancient man before us, an ending is sensed. But the end is merely the beginning. The dance of evolution has begun.

About the Authors

Lyssa Royal is an internationally recognized author, lecturer and channel living in Arizona. While studying for her B.A. degree in psychology, she developed an interest in hypnosis and learned to place herself in an altered state of consciousness for the purpose of stress management. In 1979 Lyssa and her family witnessed an extraordinary UFO sighting near their home in New Hampshire. This experience triggered an acute interest in extraterrestrial phenomena that propelled her into an indepth study of the nature of human and extraterrestrial consciousness using her channeling and intuitive abilities. Though she works frequently with extraterrestrial information, the practical application of her material is her highest priority.

Lyssa Royal has been conducting seminars and sacred site tours around the world since 1985. She has appeared on national and international television and radio and has contributed to numerous magazines. She is the author of several books published in at least seven languages including *Millennium: Tools for the Coming Changes, Preparing for Contact, Visitors from Within,* and *The Prism of Lyra: An Exploration of Human Galactic Heritage.* Lyssa is listed in *Who's Who in American Writers, Editors, and Poets.* She lives in Arizona with her husband Ron Holt and continues to write and travel worldwide.

Keith Priest is an independent researcher, author, and complementary medical therapist (acupuncture and homeopathy) living in Arizona. He studied music at Michigan State University. Through his research he has delved into ancient languages, biblical studies, anthropology, archaeology, history and religions, combining those studies with astronomy, mythology, and psychology. Though Keith has never seen a UFO (much less an extraterrestrial), his diverse studies have shown him that the ET issue is an integral piece of the puzzle that may connect them all.

ROYAL PRIEST RESEARCH
c/o PO Box 30973
Phoenix, Arizona 85046 U.S.A.
Web Site: www.royalpriest.com

Other Books by Lyssa Royal

MILLENNIUM:
Tools for the Coming Changes
by Lyssa Royal

Since the mid-1980s Lyssa Royal has been receiving groundbreaking information and teachings from the spiritual realms. For the first time ever, some of the most profound teachings that have been given through Lyssa are synthesized into book form.

Millennium intimately explores the global shift in consciousness, the inner workings of the human psyche and the nature of reality in a way that inspires readers to bring more happiness, fulfillment, and self-empowerment into their lives. *Millennium* offers instruction to those readers who wish to incorporate the teachings into their lives through simple yet effective techniques designed to shift the perception of the reader and thus their very reality itself. *Millennium* is an effective guidebook to navigate the uncharted waters of the new millennium with ease, grace, self-confidence, and an open heart.

ISBN 0-9631320-3-2, $13.95   Chinese/Croatian

PREPARING FOR CONTACT
A Metamorphosis of Consciousness
by Lyssa Royal and Keith Priest

This groundbreaking book is a combination of narrative, precisely focused channeled material and personal accounts. An inside look at the ET contact experience is given including what the human consciousness experiences during contact with an extraterrestrial and how our perceptions of reality change during contact. The authors present a breathtaking look at the contact phenomenon and its connection to the evolution of the human species.

ISBN 0-9631320-2-4, $12.95   Japanese/German/Polish

VISITORS FROM WITHIN
Extraterrestrial Contact and Species Evolution
by Lyssa Royal and Keith Priest

Second Edition! This book explores the extraterrestrial contact and abduction phenomenon in a unique and intriguing way. A combination of narrative, precisely focused channeled material and first-hand accounts, this book challenges the reader to use the abduction phenomenon as a tool for personal and planetary evolution. It will encourage you to expand your beliefs about extraterrestrial contact forever. Twenty pages have been added with new and updated info.

ISBN 1-893183-04-1, $14.95   Second Edition - 1999

THE PRISM OF LYRA
An Exploration of Human Galactic Heritage
by Lyssa Royal and Keith Priest

This introductory book examines the idea of creation in a different light. In contrast to the notion that humans are the result of creation, it explores the idea that the collective humanoid consciousness (or soul) created our universe for specific purposes. *The Prism of Lyra* then traces various developing off-planet races (such as cultures from Lyra, Sirius, Orion and the Pleiades) through their own evolution and ties them into the evolving Earth. Highlighted is the realization of our galactic interconnectedness and our shared desire to return home.

ISBN 0-9631320-0-8, $11.95   Japanese/German/Korean/Polish/Chinese/Portuguese

To Order: You may order any of the above books in the english language from your local bookstore or by sending a check or money order (in US Dollars) to Royal Priest Research, PO Box 30973, Phoenix, Arizona 85046. Please add $3.50 shipping for the first book and $1.50 for each additional book. Foreign orders, please add $7. U.S. dollars only. *Sorry, we do not accept credit card orders.*

WWW.ROYALPRIEST.COM

ACKNOWLEDGMENTS

We thank the following people for their assistance and support during the production of the original text for the First Edition of *Visitors from Within*:

Dr. Heide Davis
Stephen Davis
Paul Jaffe
Michael Lindemann
Margaret Pinyan (editing)
Stacey Vornbrock, M.A.
Col. Donald Ware (ret.)
Corey Wolfe (cover art)
Mark B. Woodhouse, Ph.D.

Our heartfelt gratitude to Granite Publishing and especially Pam and Brian for their assistance with the Second Edition, their belief in this work and their generous support.

Much appreciation and admiration is sent to the original Las Vegas, Nevada children's contactee support group.

And we sincerely thank all humans who have allowed this phenomenon to touch their lives . . .

If you would like
to see more books
by Granite Publishing,
or its imprints
Wild Flower Press or Swan•Raven & Co.
write to us at
P.O. Box 1429
Columbus, NC 28722

or call

800.366.0264

and we'll send you
a free catalog.
or visit us on the web—

http://5thworld.com/granite

Granite
Publishing

NOTES